Entrepreneurship: MY STORY, YOUR GUIDE

Sharndell Lowe
& co- authors

Copyright © 2017 Sharndell Lowe

All rights reserved.

Sharndell Lowe & co-authors

Copyright Notice

Copyright 2017, Sharndell Lowe
All rights reserved, including the right to reproduce this book or any portion thereof in any form whatsoever.

This book is designed to provide accurate and authoritative information with regard to the subject matter covered. It is sold with the understanding that there is not a professional consulting engagement. If expert advice or assistance is required, please seek a professional that may assist you.

For information on bulk orders or to have Sharndell Lowe speak at your event, contact sharndell@sharndelllowe.com

DEDICATION

To my mother Brenda, I thank you for always being there for me through the good and the bad and my two boys J. Michael and Kai for keeping me personally accountable for my life choices as your mom.

TABLE OF CONTENTS

Page 5   Sharndell Lowe- *How to Go From Discovering Your Passion to Living Your Dreams*

Page 27   Tina A. Gray- *Defiantly She*

Page 43   Christina Elkins- *Be Your Own Muse*

Page 63   Lenise Williams-*Mind(set) Over Matter*

Page 83   Osnita L. Norman- *For the Love of Resale: It's How You "Rock" It*

Page 108   Mindy P. Hobley- *I Trusted My Gut*

Page 130   Sonceria Roper- *Nurse to Entrepreneur*

Page 146   Patrina Dixon- *Phenomenally Me*

CHAPTER ONE

How to Go From Discovering Your Passion to Living Your Dreams

Sharndell Lowe

Discovery:

I have always been an entrepreneur and a 'hustler' at heart. However, my family life and my career as an Information Technology (IT) professional didn't allow for much 'me' time. I was so distracted by life that I didn't do any soul searching to discover my true God-given talents. As we know, God will get our attention when He has a plan for us. In my case, I was forced to take time out to hear what God was speaking to me as I recovered from a major surgery.

One morning I was washing my face and I felt a lump behind my ear. I ignored it for a couple of weeks before telling my mom. She told me that I should not ignore the lump another day and that I needed to see a doctor immediately. I took several tests and the results revealed that I had a benign parotic gland tumor in my face. I am so thankful to God that I listened to my mom. Test results revealed that surgery was the only option to have the tumor removed and I quickly scheduled the procedure. My surgery went well for the most part; however, my nerves scattered during the procedure causing minor paralysis on the left side of my face. I was devastated at being unable to smile, blink or feel anything. Furthermore, my doctor told me that the left side of my face would be paralyzed for six months to a year. I looked at the doctor and said, "Are you kidding me?!?" You see, my smile is who I am. I love to smile and I am always laughing, thanks to my bubbly personality. But God!! God saw differently and my face was fully functional three months following my surgery. I am a witness that God has the final say.

After the surgery, I was advised to stay at home for several weeks to allow for proper healing. During this time period, I wasn't able to move my head in a rigorous manner. That meant that I couldn't drive – so I would not be able to travel to the local bakery to satisfy my nagging sweet tooth. What was a girl to do? There was only one solution – I had to start baking. I began researching different recipes to determine what paired well with the ingredients that I had on hand in my refrigerator and pantry. At that point, I realized that all I needed were the basics (flour, baking powder, sugar, milk, eggs and butter). Let's go!! Soon my first cake was underway and the rest is history. I started baking every day and discovered that I was good at it. Baking kept me busy during those long hours while I was sitting at home recovering from my surgery. Baking fostered a way for me to be creative.

The Food Network became my version of attending culinary school. I watched every episode of Cupcake Wars, Cake Wars and Chopped. These shows encouraged me to take my baking up a notch. I became bolder with my flavor combinations. I no longer was baking just vanilla, chocolate and red velvet cupcakes. I began to pair weird flavors that would create a flavor explosion in your mouth. I shared my new creations with my neighbors, friends and family members so that I could get their feedback. I received some constructive feedback and some criticism. I welcomed it all; you see, I was trying to reach perfection with my creativity. My confidence went through the roof after several rounds of trial and error. I thought, "I can really bake!"

I realize now that if I hadn't gone through such a major surgery, I may have never discovered my passion for baking.

Lesson Learned: Sometimes, God will take you through a situation to show you His plan for your life.

ENTREPRENEURSHIP: MY STORY, YOUR GUIDE

Hobby vs Business:

- Hobby – an enjoyable activity one does during their free time not to make a profit.

- Business – one pursues an activity or makes a product to make a profit.

I wanted to share my newfound passion with everyone who would listen. I came up with a name that would represent me and my new craft: "Cupcake and a Smile"!! I then put on my marketing hat and went to work. I hired a graphic designer to create my logo, business cards and website. I defined my signature menu and began advertising my product and services. I became a marketing 'queen' and before I knew it, I was baking for every occasion possible where my sweet treats were the 'perfect' fit. I couldn't believe it; Cupcake and a Smile became my home-based bakery.

I would bake late at night and early in the morning and then make deliveries before and after work and sometimes during my lunch break and Saturday mornings. I quickly learned the power of word-of-mouth. I was taking orders weekly from my friends and from friends of my friends for a variety of occasions, including office, school and personal events. Not only did my customers enjoy my product, but they loved my customer service even more. I had literally joined Team "No Days Off" and Team "No Sleep".

The demand for my product grew exponentially over the first six months of operation and I was forced to make a decision. Do I continue operating my God-given passion as a hobby or as a business? I realized that where there is sufficient demand, a hobby can develop into a business. To have a successful business, I had to consider the idea of turning my hobby into a full-time career. But was I really ready to make this type of commitment? Did I really want to give up my six-figure income for a 'hobby'?

I immediately went into prayer and asked God to guide my steps for the steps of a righteous man are ordered by Christ. My brain went into an overload of questions. "Is now a good time to go from a 'hobby' to a 'business'?" If so, the next question was "Can I manage a healthy balance among the demands of my family life, career and business?"

In order to answer these questions, I had to do my due diligence. I knew that a clear sign of progressing from a hobby to a business is all about profit. In order to assure that I could make a profit, I had to decipher if there was a 'true' opportunity, regardless of the current demand. I began to research opportunities to prove my concept. One thing that I knew for sure was that there is a growing preference for homemade desserts over desserts available from the grocery store. I also knew that consumers who prefer homemade desserts don't have time to make them. My business could tackle this need because not only could I make homemade desserts, but I could deliver them too.

Once I clearly defined the opportunity, I had to decipher how I would solve the problem if I decided to go from operating my passion as a hobby to operating my passion as a business. What are my alternatives for the problem that I have identified? Do I purchase a food truck so I could provide both service and deliveries or do I lease retail space? At the end of the day, I knew that I wasn't ready to give up my full-time job. So, after exploring both alternatives and weighing the pros and cons of each, I decided to purchase a Food Truck. Let's make this happen!!

Cupcake and a Smile was now a business and I was officially a bakerpreneur. The next step was to write my business plan. My plan had to be solid because I had to prove my concept to a lender so that I would be granted funds to purchase a food truck and also have money left over to operate. It took me about eight months to get my business plan just right. I was advised to seek funding from local lenders affiliated with the Small Business Administration (SBA) instead of going to a bank. I took that advice and was approved for an SBA loan. I was so excited and didn't waste any time. I got my employer identification number (EIN), found a vendor to build out a truck for me, and another vendor to wrap my truck. I purchased supplies needed for individual cupcake packaging and storage and I purchased insurance. I reached out to other food trucks as a network opportunity to find locations where I could park my truck to serve customers and I also picked their brains about lessons they'd learned. After my truck was ready for the streets, I went to the health department and purchased my health permit. Whoop! Whoop! I passed inspection. Before I knew it, I was operating "Sweetness" (my name for my food truck) part-time every Friday at office buildings and every Saturday at food parks.

I absolutely loved operating my new food truck business. I was still scheduling two to three dessert deliveries during the week, all while working my full-time job. I was literally SUPER WOMAN, a true mompreneur.

I had to consider many things before officially launching my business. Here are a few things to consider when you decide to turn your hobby into a business:

1. Identify the opportunity.

Assess the problem and determine if you will make a profit from satisfying the need.

2. Test the market.

Make sure that there is a demand for your offerings and listen to your customers.

3. Identify and weigh alternatives.

Be careful not to jump to solutions. Have several options.

4. Make a plan.

Write your business plan and document the solution to the problem.

5. Network.

Start by reaching out to other entrepreneurs in the same industry. Pick their brains for lessons learned. Use social media as a marketing tool to create awareness and to gain insights about your target market.

6. Be competitive.

Differentiate your product at a good price point.

7. **Operate your business.**

Set goals, track progress and take corrective actions.

Turning your hobby into a business is a great way to become your own boss. It is so important to have a solid plan before starting your business. If you don't plan for it, it won't happen. Take the time to write a robust business plan. Make sure that your business offers goods and/or services that solve a problem. And remember that process improvement is continuous.

Write this sentence and fill in the blanks: The purpose of my business is to _____ so that_____because_____.

Lesson Learned: Put in the work and God will do the rest.

Food Truck to Brick-and-Mortar Location

My food truck was my pilot and it allowed me to build my brand. By operating my food truck, I was able to build invaluable relationships with my customers and they quickly became my best source for product feedback. I gathered their input on what they liked and didn't like as well as what they wanted to see next from Cupcake and a Smile. I was also able to gain an understanding of where a large percentage of my customer base lived and worked and how far they would be willing to travel to purchase my desserts.

I thought, "If I could successfully operate my food truck and create a loyal following, then one day I would be well positioned to open a brick-and-mortar location." Opening a brick-and-mortar was my ultimate goal. With an actual physical location, I would be able to meet the demand of my customers in a manner that would be convenient for them to get my sweet treats of choice at any time.

My customers loved my desserts and I came to believe that if they followed me to my food truck stops, surely they would follow me to my anchored location. My new customers boosted my confidence by continuously asking me "Where are you located?" and "Can we get your product on demand?". My loyal customers really boosted my confidence by telling me, "You need to open a brick-and-mortar store." I listened to my customers, heard the demand for my product loud and clear, and knew that business expansion was the next logical step.

While business expansion was beginning to get underway, I had to face a major road block. I was still working full-time as an informational technology business analyst/project manager and I still was not ready to give up my six-figure income. Although I wasn't ready to jump, my inner voice told me that it was time for me to step out on faith. Have you ever had a nagging feeling inside that just wouldn't go away? What is that feeling? Just in case you didn't know, it's the Holy Spirit. I had this nagging sense that wouldn't quit, no matter how hard I tried to suppress it. The tugging at my gut just kept getting louder and louder. No matter the discomfort I was feeling, I still would not listen because I was not about to take a leap of faith. To be quite honest, I was afraid of the unknown. I didn't want to quit my job and risk not being able to take care of my two young boys.

So, although I wasn't ready to give up my 9 a.m. – 5 p.m. full-time comfort zone, I had to begin planning. I knew that something was about to happen; I just didn't know how or when. So, I lived in the 'NOW' expecting God to work His miracles. Even if my plan wasn't His plan, I wanted to be ready, I had to have a plan. Developing my next move calmed my Spirit, but it didn't quiet it. So, because of God's perfect timing, He had to step in once again and force me to move. But this time, He literally pushed me off the cliff. The IT project that I was working on was cancelled. Not only was I laid off, but my entire team was let go. Looking towards God, I saw this as a blessing. It may seem crazy to some, but it was a blessing for me. I was working as a contractor so I didn't have any benefits to follow my final paycheck and I didn't care. Getting laid off was confirmation that God was about to do something GREAT in my life. My dreams of having my own brick-and-mortar store were about to come true. I didn't even think about looking for another job; instead, I looked for a bakery location and began operating my dessert truck full-time.

I received so much criticism from people in my outer circle who didn't understand" the vision." I didn't care what the naysayers had to say because I realized that not everyone will get it and I was okay with it. I knew that I wasn't a 'formal' well-trained baker, nor was I financially set up or the smartest in this industry. However, what I am is ambitious and determined and I am willing to go the extra mile and beyond to get the job done. More importantly, God had given me PEACE. You see, that nagging feeling that I spoke of earlier in this chapter was now quiet.

Here are some steps to take when you decide to go from a food truck (or any mobile business) to a brick-and-mortar storefront:

Research locations. The "right" location is the key to operating a successful business. For starters, you should choose a location in a high-traffic area that has easy access and plenty of parking. You must then examine the demographics for the area and evaluate foot traffic at nearby establishments. It is also important to know who your direct competitors are within the proximity of your desired location.

Know your numbers and watch your finances. Get ready to list out your upcoming expenses, which in my case included: kitchen equipment and supplies; furniture and décor for the service area; signage; start-up costs; insurance; more staff; and more food ingredients for baking. It is also key to understand the difference between your variable and your fixed costs. Understand your potential slow periods and have a contingency plan in place to help you overcome those periods. Most importantly, set aside money for a rainy day.

Strategically plan your menus and allocate kitchen and food truck resources. Plan your menu strategically to align with the needs of your demographics. Some menu items that work on your food truck may or may not work at your brick-and-mortar location. Be prepared to make changes as necessary. It may be beneficial to expand your product offerings which will increase your repeat business. The key is to satisfy the needs and wants of your newly acquired customers. Keep an open mind to what they are telling you.

Your brick-and-mortar kitchen will likely double as your food truck's commissary. Be mindful that you are operating two entities that will require adding more staff with more responsibilities. Scheduling your staff successfully will be a key component of your day-to-day operations.

How will you operate your truck now that you have a brick-and-mortar location? Opening a brick-and-mortar storefront that operates year-round may mean changing the purpose of your food truck. Your truck can continue with the same operation model or you can choose to decrease daily routes and focus on catering special events and making deliveries. Regardless of its function, your food truck still will be an invaluable billboard.

Lesson Learned: When God is for us, who can be against us.

Running a Brick-and-Mortar Operation

Operation – Activities involved in the day-to-day

functions of the business that are conducted for the purpose of generating profits.

It is time to operate. The hard work begins now that the doors are open for business. All entrepreneurs want to be successful; however, success does not happen overnight and it is not guaranteed. Running and scaling a successful business requires flexibility, good planning and organizational skills, and a solid foundation of processes and procedures.

There are three nuggets that I learned from Marcus Lemonis' television show, "The Profit." He said that building a solid operation is all about the three P's: *process*, *people* and *product*. For instance, I've found that it is so important to have proper documentation for everything as it relates to business operations. I display all processes that my employees need to be successful in a common area; that way, they are reminded of these processes on a daily basis. I have also learned that in order to have a consistent product, I have to give my employees what they need to deliver a successful product. For example, we have weekly meetings to discuss upcoming events and orders, process improvement opportunities and concerns.

Here are some of the steps that I follow while operating my business:

1. **Stay organized**
Organization is key to a successful business. A good way to stay organized is to create a robust to-do list each day. Prioritize your to-do list by examining each item with the question, "Will I lose money if I don't complete this item today?"

2. **Keep detailed financial records**
All successful businesses are aware of their financials. Most businesses face financial challenges and endure mistakes at some point. By staying on top of your finances, you will know when potential challenges arise and when to execute your contingency plan to mitigate those challenges. At the end of the day, You Must Know Your NUMBERS!!

3. **Stay focused**

Just because your doors open for business doesn't mean that you're going to make money immediately. Therefore, stay focused on your short-term goals. It is also important to stay focused on your customers. Your customers are your key to success. Happy customers become repeat customers and they will bring new customers with them.

4. Provide excellent customer service

Great customer service is the best way to increase revenue. Talk to your customers and listen to their feedback. Make sure that you understand their needs and provide products and services that are better than what your competitors offer.

5. Be Consistent

You have to consistently keep doing what is necessary to be successful day in and day out. By implementing best practices, you will create long-term positive habits that will help you make money in your business.

6. Hire the right people

Definitely make sure you hire exceptional people who are skilled and have a solid work ethic and pleasant personalities. Make sure their assigned tasks are aligned with their strengths to mitigate resentment and poor performance. More importantly, value your employees and treat them as team players so that they want to be attached to the business. At the end of the day, they influence your success in business.

7. Create awareness

Advertise your business. Hand out business cards, share photos on various social media platforms, create a signature item and network with other business owners. You will not experience success if no one knows your business exists.

8. Keep advancing

Never stop setting goals. Document your "lessons learned" so that you can improve your processes.

9. Never give up

You will face many obstacles and financial challenges. When they come, don't be afraid to face them head on with a plan to defeat them. There is a saying that goes, "Love what you do and the money will follow." Stay in the fight and your efforts will pay off.

10. Lastly, take care of you

Take time off to recharge yourself and make your family a priority. Nurture your physical, emotional, mental and spiritual health.

*Lesson Learned: I can do **all** things through Christ who strengthens me!!*

So, what's next for Cupcake and a Smile? I am now working to perfect my business model so that I can expand. I have identified that a growing need for Cupcake and a Smile exists and I have generated several alternatives to satisfy the demand. The possibilities are endless now that I have done most of the hard work. I am ready for the ride.

ABOUT THE AUTHOR

Sharndell Lowe has recently been known as a baker by those around her. After years of encouragement from friends and family, Sharndell opened Cupcake and a Smile as a business in the fall of 2011. For the first couple of years, Sharndell operated solely as a catering business. While working full time, Sharndell built up her business by baking at night and on weekends. By 2013, she was ready to purchase a food truck to increase her visibility and maximize the potential of the business. By January of 2016, she opened her first brick-and-mortar storefront in Richmond, TX where she operates 5 days a week and has 2 part-time employees.

Sharndell's business model focuses on serving cupcakes that are so delicious, they make you smile. Excellent customer service, product differentiation and a good price point sets Cupcake and a Smile apart from other food trucks and bakeries in Houston and surrounding areas. Sharndell strives to create an ongoing relationship with each customer that begins with a simple introduction and ends with the tasty treat.

Customer satisfaction can certainly attest to the success of Cupcake and a Smile. Sharndell's business has grown mainly through word-of-mouth referrals from her loyal customers. Through dedication and working hard, Sharndell has been able to grow her business.

As a business owner, Sharndell is completely dedicated to creating and serving a quality product. For her, "the happiness that results from satisfying customers makes the early morning and late-night baking worthwhile."

Stay in touch with Sharndell:
www.SharndellLowe.com
www.cupcakeandasmile.com
Facebook: www.facebook.com/cupcakeandasmile
Instagram: @cupcakeandasmile
Twitter: @ccandasmile

CHAPTER TWO
DEFIANTLY SHE

Tina A. Gray

My Industry:

My Industry is business consulting. Specifically, my company provides accounting and tax services, complimented by financial advisory support for small business owners. Many people start their own businesses and learn as they go, and I am all for that kind of confidence and action. It is usually when they start receiving letters in the mail from the Internal Revenue Service or other tax agencies that they realize they need help. Most small businesses cannot afford a full-time in-house CFO to handle the financial matters, deal with the bankers, negotiate lines of credit, manage the flow of capital, and most of all, meet all the tax filing deadlines required. So, my business provides all of these services on an outsourced basis, and it's Tag Pro Resources to the rescue!

I have been running the business for so many years and helped so many business owners get caught up, stay compliant, get fees waived, and more, that the inflow of work is continuous, maintaining itself with current clients and client referrals. As the years have gone by, I realize I have been able to achieve my goals of being independent, an entrepreneur, a business owner, and having a sense of personal success. I did it from the ground up, solo, bootstrapped, hungry, and hustling. I have dealt with fear, doubt, anxiety, uncertainty, and have also experienced great joy, accomplishment, and unlimited career and personal fulfillment.

After reflecting on my journey and my own career, I decided to share my story with others. Welcome to my second business endeavor, Her Success LLC. Her Success is an organization that celebrates women in business, provides speaking engagements, collaborates in written and editorial productions, and most importantly, *empowers* women. I invite you to celebrate the stories in this book and also be on the lookout for the upcoming release of my next production—*The Secret to Her Success*!

My Story:

My story is probably a lot like anyone else's story. My parents divorced when I was young and I never knew my father. My mother raised my brother and me on her own. We collected green stamps. I wore my brother's hand-me-downs that had already been purchased at a second-hand store or given to us. I remember we ate lots of egg sandwiches, which to this day I still love. I could have eggs for breakfast, lunch, and dinner and be just as happy as if I had a four-course dinner. Okay, I take that back, a four-course dinner can be pretty good—it's the service that comes with it that makes it such an indulgence.

We grew up in the less expensive areas of town, and we couldn't afford all the things we wanted. My mother spent many sleepless nights worrying about money, but we never went hungry. My mother worked most of her life as secretary at a local Catholic church. My brother and I spent our summers on the farm with family. We had a good life, but it was clear we didn't measure high on the social scale of wealth. One of the first things I realized as a child was that we were poor, and that was just the way it was.

I remember one day at my grandparents' house in which I was playing on the porch with the some of the kittens that seemed to always be around. Looking out the screen window from his seat at the kitchen table, my grandfather asked me what I was going to be when I grew up. He said, "Are you going to be a secretary like your mom?" I was probably seven or eight years old at the time. I stopped and thought about it and responded, "No grandpa, I am going to *have* a secretary." He wasn't impressed. He'd worked as a butcher at the local meat market all of his life. Who did I think I was, thinking I was going to be somebody? I suppose the biggest obstacle I overcame growing up was that the world simply wasn't expecting very much from me. But *I* was.

My mother's boss was the priest at the Catholic church where she worked all those years. He wanted to make sure my brother and I both had a Catholic school education, and he set aside money for us to attend the local Catholic high schools. I suppose we were like the children he never had, and he wanted the best for us. I went to school with lots of the local wealthy girls, and it was intimidating. They all had their expensive clothes and expensive cars. I was just happy to have a few dollars to put gas in my car. People often told me I could be anything I wanted to be. But if that was true, why wasn't everybody what they wanted to be? I appreciated the kind words, and I wasn't sure how I was going to do it. But I was going to figure it out.

When it came time to apply for colleges, I knew I wanted to get out of the small town I was in and applied to a university in the closest big city, Dallas. I didn't know much about colleges. I had heard of Southern Methodist University (SMU) and it seemed to be a good college, so I applied there. I remember one day coming home from high school with my mother and driving into the car port. We had one of those small metal mailboxes with the top flip cover, and as we drove up we noticed a large envelope sticking out of it. We could see that the envelope was from SMU, and my mother said, "Well, you got into SMU," partly in disbelief, and partly in fear of how we were going to pay for it.

Why I Decided to Become An Entrepreneur:

Why did I decide to become an entrepreneur? I got tired of working for The Man. Such a cliché line, but it's true. One of my favorite quotes is by Madeleine Albright: "There is plenty of room in this world for mediocre men. There is no room for mediocre women." She is right. Mediocre men are everywhere. Just drive through downtown Dallas around lunchtime, and you will see them all jollying out to lunch with the boys. You won't see very many women. The women are all inside, working through their lunch breaks, having a snack bar or protein drink at their desks, hoping to show how dedicated they are to their work and their company, while their bosses all head out to lunch. As far as we have come, ladies, we have so much further to go.

ENTREPRENEURSHIP: MY STORY, YOUR GUIDE

I think back to some of my former bosses, I used to wonder to myself—how in the world did someone like that get put in charge? Now, to be fair, I have had both male and female supervisors that I have greatly admired and learned very much from. I appreciated the ones who saw my value, recognized my work, and financially rewarded me for my contributions to the organization. But the greatly admired bosses were definitely in the minority. What I started doing early on in my career was watching and learning. I watched how business was conducted on a daily basis—who made the decisions and why certain decisions were made. Who got the promotions and who didn't. Who got invited to lunch and who didn't. Who sat in on the important meetings and who didn't. When you pay real close attention, you realize it's not terribly complex. It was more about whoever the boss liked, and the boss was typically male, so the favorites were typically his male cronies. Most decisions were made without careful thought, without considering the long term financial impact on the company, and without thinking about how employee morale would be affected. And then most of these "decision makers" would all take off at 3pm to head to the golf course....Really?? Yes, really.

Right Place, Wrong Gender

I remember when I worked for the Dallas Cowboys Football Club. It was in the late 90's. I really loved working there—great benefits, season tickets, a pension plan, not to mention all the other great perks. But the one thing I learned was that I may have been at the right place, but I was the wrong gender. If I had been a man with a degree from the University of Arkansas (where the Cowboys owner graduated from), I would have almost certainly qualified for a six-figure salary. But I was a woman with a business degree from Southern Methodist University, and I had the student loans to prove it. I was also working on a master's degree at night, hoping that someone would eventually recognize my value to the organization. They didn't. I was mostly recognized for always having a smile on my face or for being a great team player. Sometimes I even got an "atta girl" for my problem-solving skills or for working 80 hours a week. I was sharp, hardworking, and making and saving the organization some serious money. And then I would be casually and routinely overlooked when it came time for the annual bonuses and big promotions. I was eventually recruited away from the Cowboys. After six years with the team, I could see the glass ceiling, and mama didn't raise no fool! After leaving, I worked for a local accounting firm and later a private equity firm. I enjoyed working at the other companies but never felt like my talents were being fully utilized, recognized, or rewarded.

And then one day, it hit me. The only person who was ever really going to pay me what I was worth, who really saw the value of what I was bringing to the table, and who had the ability and intent to compensate me appropriately... was ME! So that was it, I would start my own business. Look out world, here I come! I was smart, talented, and had been underutilized my entire career, and I could do this! I think. Sure I can, right? Yes, it turns out, I actually could. It also turned out that the only person who really needed to believe in me, was me.

How I Funded My Start-up:
Did Somebody Say Credit Card?

Once I decided to start my own business, I knew it would take some time to gain clients and establish a steady flow of income. I was leaving a career where I was making close to six figures, and I knew walking away from that was a risk. But I wasn't happy with my current situation and I was the only one who could change it. This is important to note: When you decide you are going to take a chance on yourself, it's all or nothing. No safety nets, no side gigs, no self-doubt, no counting on family to pay your bills. It can be scary, but you have to go ALL in. So, I did. I calculated the rent, the car note, the groceries, and so forth, and figured what my worst-case scenario would be to stay in business working for myself. After doing the math, I figured that if I could bring in about $3,000 a month, it would be just enough to cover current bills and I could stay in business for myself. It may mean living on ramen noodles for a while, but that was ok. I had come from little or nothing, so I knew how to survive on little or nothing. I waited for the annual bonus at my current job then respectfully gave my notice. The bonus would keep me afloat for maybe two months and allow me to invest in business cards, a basic website, and attend some networking events. I thought surely I would have paying clients within two months. Surely I would, wouldn't I?

But it took me longer than two months. I had clients, but I was also funding my business with credit cards. I ran up about $25,000 in credit card debt the first two years. But in year three, all the late nights, the hard work, the professional presentation, and the belief in myself paid off. I had doubled my revenue year over year, three years in a row. I recommend you stay focused and be keenly aware of where you are spending your money. Don't sign the three-year office lease on your first day in business. Don't commit to a four-year equipment lease for something that may or may not help you in your journey. Research the companies you do business with, such as vendors and customers, see if they are integrity based businesses. As for your business resources, talk to other small business owners and find out what they are using for industry software, phone/fax/internet, part-time or shared office space, free or affordable marketing options, and other resources. Be efficient and know when to outsource the things you don't know how to do. Don't spend 12 hours trying to fix your computer when you can pay a professional for one hour to fix it for you. Find a legal mind to review your contracts, rather than trying to become your own attorney. Find a great marketing resource that can present you in a professional light with three hours of work, when it would take you three days. And take the chances that don't cost you a dime. Make the call you are not sure you should make. Visit the business owner you would like to know more about. And when you start taking on clients, get paid up front. Seriously. Sometimes all you have to do is ask. You will be surprised how much people will do for you and with you.

Marketing Tips:

Relationships, Relationships, Relationships

I have maintained a strong network of connections in my career, and lots of them are women in my industry and related industries (finance, accounting, banking, insurance). Relationships really are the key. One of the most critical elements in building your own business is to have a strong network of friends, associates, contacts, and professional relationships. The connections that are going places, not the ones that are just fun to hang out with. I networked like crazy my first two years in business. Along the way, I established relationships and connections, ones that I never knew would be the ones that would refer the $50,000 or $75,000 clients to me in the future.

Until you can fill your books with paying clients, volunteer your business services at a local non-profit. I said *non*-profit, not *for*-profit. Never give your products or services away to other for-profits. I am not talking about samples, I am talking about what you expect people to pay you for. I have found that working with non-profits is a great marketing strategy. It is an excellent way to stay productive and test your skills at being self-employed. It's also a great way to get your name, business, and product or services out there. Plus, when you do great work with a local non-profit, you can ask them to provide a reference for your future paying clients. It's a win-win.

Stay relevant. If you cannot do it on your own, hire someone who can. Today we live in a whirlwind of social media. I don't know the rules; I just know there is a machine grinding behind every tweet, post, like, and share. So I tweet, post, like, and share! I try to stay measured in my media. Personally, I try not to let an emotional day take over the tone of my social media accounts. But if you are having a particularly inspiring day (or even a particularly low moment), as long as you are sincere, inoffensive, and authentic in your post, you have no apologies to make later. We are all just people. And like minds tend to come together with other like minds.

Stay connected. My business is 95% referral-based, so I recommend staying connected to all current and former clients, all prospects, and all connections. Even the ones who may have declined your services or products in the past. I speak from experience when I say you would be surprised how many people come back around once they realize they made the wrong decision. They lost time and money on the wrong choice, and now they will give just about *anything* to get back on your calendar and work with you. Don't take advantage—take care—and they will become loyal clients and refer other clients to you.

Be scrutinizing. You will cross paths with all kinds of people, some of whom lack ethics or scruples. The great thing about being the boss is that you don't have to work with people you don't want to work with. Always subscribe to a professional demeanor, but never sacrifice your character, your reputation, or your valuable time to help someone who doesn't value your work or is looking to cut corners at your expense. You will naturally be drawn to work with people who have your shared values, so trust that those relationships will present themselves. These are the people you will have the most success working with, and it will come naturally. So, trust your instinct when it comes to choosing your clients. If that little voice in the back of your mind says something doesn't feel right—walk away.

In conclusion, if you are considering starting your own business, think about the talents and abilities that come naturally to you. Find something you are good at and hone those skills. Choose something that you enjoy. And feel free to color outside of the lines! If there is something you have always dreamed of doing as a career, do it! Be smart about it, prepare yourself for the ups and downs, do your research, streamline your vision and most importantly, put your thoughts into action. And don't be afraid to ask other professionals for their feedback or help. Surround yourself with positive people. And simply believe in yourself. I have a secret to share with you: *The world is waiting for you!*

ABOUT THE AUTHOR

Tina is an accomplished business owner, mentor, speaker and author. She has been empowering women for over 15 years. She has a BBA in Finance and an MSA in Accounting from Southern Methodist University. She lives in Dallas and is a native of the great state of Texas.

Stay in touch with Tina:
www.tagpros.net

Instagram: @hersuccess123

CHAPTER THREE

Be Your Own Muse

Christina Elkins

My name is Christina Elkins and I am a child of God, a wife, a mother, an employee, and a CEO of a digital marketing firm. I know it all seems like a lot, and sometimes it is, but I believe that if you have a dream or a goal you should go for it. Although I hold a bachelor's degree in communications and a Master's Degree in Internet Marketing, I currently work in corporate America for a hospital. I once heard a financial coach say that it is important to monetize your skills in order to generate an income. Therefore, I decided to start a Digital Marketing agency that specializes in online advertising and marketing solutions.

The faces of advertising and marketing are changing rapidly. There are thousands of business owners out there trying to keep up the pace. I have a specific set of skills that helps business owners reach their online marketing goals in order to generate more revenue. When I am not working with clients, I write music and produce a podcast about things that I am passionate about.

My goal is to share my story with you so that you can see that it is possible to overcome setbacks and obstacles in order to achieve your goals. You are not a result of your past or current circumstances. Entrepreneurship is hard.

ENTREPRENEURSHIP: MY STORY, YOUR GUIDE

There will be times when you do not have any money. Things will seem difficult, and you will want to give up. But you can't give up because you are unique, and there is no one else like you. No one else can do what you can do quite like you. The world needs you to bring your dreams to pass as you pursue excellence on every level.

Although I have reached success, it has been a journey. I still remember being dropped off at the homeless shelter in my teenage years. At that time in my life I was very rambunctious, to say the least.

I grew up in Houston, TX. My parents met each other in Cleveland, OH where they were both born and raised. They migrated to the south and never looked back. My parents divorced when I was nine. My father was diagnosed with Multiple Sclerosis. By the time he was 36, he was admitted to a nursing home. This left me in a bad position. I lived with him at the time. So, when he became displaced it put me in a bad situation. I had to live with various friends and family members. Often times crashing on people's couches and floors. At one point, I found myself living in the projects in Cleveland, OH. In spite of my surroundings, I always knew that there was something better for me. Many people tried to define me based on my circumstances. But I was determined to rise above my environment I got through that difficult time in my life and went on to graduate high school and college and secure a job in Corporate America. I did not allow my past to define me. I had a goal, I worked hard and I refused to give up. The fact that I am in this position in life sometimes still feels like a dream; I have to pinch myself at times.

I worked hard and achieved my goal of obtaining my Bachelor's degree and securing a great position in Corporate America. Although I was successful in achieving my goal, there was still something inside of me that yearned for more. As "luck" would have it, my cousin who worked at the same company, and I were laid off. We acknowledged that as a sign for us to finally use our skills and expertise to create a business that we loved. I remember the day that we sat down and decided to create our one stop digital marketing company. We outlined the principles of the business and launched a business in which we offer website development, business cards, business plans, marketing plans and commercials. In this chapter I would like to share with you a few principles which have been the foundation for our success in this industry. Below are some of the principles upon which we have found success as it relates to digital marketing and search engine optimization.

Finding your Zone:

Before we talk about anything, we will first discuss the importance of finding one's own lane. My intention is not to put you in a box. Some people have one talent and others have many talents. It is not about how many talents you have; it is about having a strategy and maximizing your potential. The objective is to get you to align your talents in proper position with your ambition so that you can find success.

My questions to you are: What is the one thing you would do without getting paid? Do you have a dream or an idea that won't go away? Have you ever thought to yourself, I wish I could sustain my own income? Well if your answer is yes, then you should keep reading. Once you identify what you do well, you need to focus and channel your energy appropriately. For me it has always been about bringing great ideas into fruition. In my early 20's I became interested and passionate about web design. Although I did not have formal training, I was able to successfully navigate through the web design world. I found my zone and I began to create a strategy for my business.

My cousin and I are different and at times it

becomes difficult operating a business with a family member. We have been able to figure out our roles and get past any different opinions that we may have. Overcoming those obstacles became easier once we learned how to stay in our zone. When one learns to stay in their zone and their lane, they can thrive beyond the circumstances. We mastered what we were each good at and remained true to that. Finding our individual zones gave us each the ability to live beyond our wildest dreams. We recognized one another's strengths and weaknesses and were able to develop a business that we love. Finding your zone will include being honest with yourself about who you were born to be.

Focus, Planning, Consistency:

Focus, planning and Consistency are all powerful tools. If utilized correctly they can be a sure- fire recipe for success.

Now that you have an idea about what it is you want to do, it is time for you to focus. Before you dive into your new exploit you have to mentally prepare yourself for the journey ahead. Visualize yourself achieving your goals and aspirations. Visualizing yourself where you want to be helps you to prepare yourself for obstacles before they occur. Yes, there will be obstacles; however, you will be mentally prepared to persevere! Remember that the road to success is a marathon and not a sprint. Therefore, you will need these next three tools in order to get where you want to be.

Planning is an essential part of business. Regardless of the industry you enter, you need to sit down and write out a plan. Your plan should cover the origin of your business, your marketing plan, a budget, financial projections, etc. If you are a good writer you can research and create a plan yourself. However, if writing is not one of your strong suits you can hire someone to do it for you. A business plan seems like a small detail, but it can really save you a lot of time and money in the long run. When you take the time out to write a plan you have a chance to visualize where you want your company to go. This can help you organize, (and remember) your thoughts. Planning is something that I really struggled with initially. I can't tell you how many times I have had phone conferences without writing down my ideas. I learned from my errors and was able to become a stronger entrepreneur because of my mistakes.

I encourage you to put your vision and your plan to paper. Doing so will really help you set and achieve your goals. Not big on writing? Use your cell phone to record your thoughts. When you are accustomed to multitasking, you tend to let some things fall by the wayside. However, if you write them down you can have a system in place to remember every brilliant idea and task that you have. Writing everything down cohesively and having a plan is important because doing so can potentially give you the opportunity to get funding. When you seek a grant or a private loan, if you have a plan people will be more willing to invest in you. No one is going to give funding to someone that does not have a plan. People want to know what you will be doing with the money. If you have a plan, you will be prepared for grants, investors, and loans.

It is also important for you to remember to refrain from placing limits on your plans. Do not make the mistake of thinking too small. Always dream and plan for bigger. The worst thing that an entrepreneur can do it to place a limit on how far they can go. The worst thing you can do is have a wonderful product with a limited perspective. This can potentially stunt your growth as a business. The Internet has made it so easy to expand. I never thought that I would be doing a commercial voiceover in Georgia for someone in Alabama. However, once we utilized the power of the internet and began to see clients from different cities and states, that is when I knew that things were really beginning to take off. But it also made me realize how powerful technology is. There are so many tools out there that can help you get the word out about you company. The internet forces you to think big!

Consistency:

It doesn't matter if your marketing budget is $200 or $20,000. You still need to figure out a way to remain consistent. Whether you are producing a commercial for your local market or a huge cable network, there are ways to make it work for you. Social media has made it easy for companies to build platforms and connect with a detailed audience. The cheapest way to get an organic following is through content marketing. This could be as simple as posting a few times a day to an existing social media account or it could be as complex as creating intentional blog posts on a regular basis. Consistency could be the difference between paying for a pay per click campaign and creating one over time with content. There are many websites out there that have managed to obtain an organic following. However, keep in mind that most of these sites have been consistently providing content for several years. Consistency is key!

Focus:

Everything that you have envisioned for your company is totally possible. You can reach every goal and bask in the success that you have worked so hard to attain. With that being said just know that it is going to take an insane amount of focus in order to get where you are trying to go. If you are a seasoned entrepreneur, this information is nothing new. If you are a budding entrepreneur, you know that the road ahead of you is one that requires a lot of work. Either way you are aware of the fact that nothing replaces hard work. It's funny because just as I was writing about focus, I began to get distracted. Nonetheless, it is important for you to focus on your efforts to plan and remain consistent. I'm not sure what your objectives are: opening a business, getting higher conversions, a specific sales goal, engagement, or it could be to expand your audience. Whatever the case is just know that it will take a lot of time and focus to get there.

Business Plan vs Marketing Plans:

Okay so you either have a template or you've got someone to complete your business plan. You are almost through and you have now reached a bump in the road. You get to the marketing plan portion of your plan and you are stumped. Now what? Essentially the marketing plan is something that is included within the business plan. However, an insane amount of intensity, research and grit is needed for the marketing plan. It's great to have a good idea. However, if no one knows about it, it doesn't really matter. A great marketing plan can help a startup reach new heights. You don't have to have a million dollars but you do need to be willing to invest. A small marketing budget is better than no budget at all. Here are a few tips that will help you implement your marketing plan.

How to Market on a Budget:

Many people feel as though it is very difficult to have a realistic marketing strategy due to their current budget. I have a friend who owns a non-profit organization. She has a company that provides mental health services for the community. She once held an event that was tailored for young disadvantaged African- American men. The event featured male figures who were prominent in the community. Each of these men were successful in their own right. However, no one came to the event because people were not aware of it. As a result, my friend spent money on refreshments, as well as other expenses, and only two young men showed up. If she had a proper strategy, she would have reached her objective. Understanding one's consumer persona is important because it allows you to hone in on a very specific group. This is important because it can be a major key when it comes to choosing the right strategy. There are tools out there that allow business owners to hone in on specific groups.

Content Marketing:

I remember when I first started out building my business. Ironically, we all have to start somewhere. I struggled with the things that most business owners struggle with: finding clients and engaging my audience. So, I began to do what I had to do, I created content. It took a while, but eventually I was able to increase my organic ranking on Google. This is important because an organic ranking can save money in the long run. As I continued to create and engage in content that matched my demographic, I was able to attract the right type of clientele.

Content marketing is something that can be painful at first, but it will all be worth it! There are companies with an organic following that creates SEO naturally. Some of these keywords are worth thousands of dollars per month; however, the company attracts traffic organically simply by remaining consistent. We all hear stories about blogs that turn into books or bloggers that blow up. Just know that unless you have a close relationship with a high- profile celebrity, you may not find success over night. You will likely find your success by contributing content. Content marketing is successful when an individual becomes a source for information within a specific niche. The goal is to become a hot spot in a specific field. You want to be the answer to a very specific and detailed problem that people can find online easily. The goal is to create as many organic links as possible and direct them toward your brand. If you do this consistently you will be easily accessible to your audience.

People may not respond at first but if you remain consistent you will see results. If you remain consistent people will begin to show up expecting to see the content they have grown to enjoy. When my cousin and I first started our company, we were faced with struggling to develop a community of clientele online. In order to combat this struggle, we posted to our social media pages every week in order to make sure that we were connecting with the audience. After a while, it became easier for us to connect with our audience. We built a network and community of individuals with common interests, which over time converted to sales.

One way we have been able to remain consistent, save time and save energy, is by planning our content ahead of time. One way to do this is to utilize tools such as Hootsuite, an app for scheduling social media posts ahead of time. Another thing that we do and encourage you to implement is to use an old-fashioned calendar! Take out a calendar and look ahead to see industry trends and plan sales, clearances, events and contests ahead of time. Remember to always think from an executive's perspective when it comes to social media. Don't get caught up in what is going on around you. Use tunnel vision in order to make efforts to create ads and content that will help promote your business.

Listen to Your Audience:

One of the major benefits of having social media is the opportunity to listen to what your audience has to say. Platforms such as Instagram and Twitter make it easy to know what people are thinking. Just a few months ago people were boycotting Shea Moisture for a campaign that they released. Social media helped the company hear what their audience was saying about their commercial. The backlash from the commercial was both detrimental and informative. The company was able to release an apology for all parties that were affected. This is why it is so important to listen to one's audience. Doing so can give you an edge on the competition. It can also make it easier for you to attract their attention when it comes to creating campaigns. In order to solve a problem, one must first acknowledge the problem. Therefore, listening to your audience warrants the opportunity for your business to become the solution, thereby adding value to your brand.

SEO and Social Media Marketing Tips:

When I first started my company, I had to start from scratch. I had no followers and no one knew that my company existed. As I began to post and blog I was able to pique the interest of my ideal client. I utilized hashtags, social media posts, and organic SEO strategies in order to raise awareness about the brand. I noticed that the more I posted, the higher the search engine ranking. I also noticed a decline in my SEO results whenever I pulled back on the social media posts. One of the biggest lessons that I learned was the it is important for me to post in order to maintain a high ranking.

More and more people are choosing to do business online; Search Engine Optimization has been vital to my business. Over the years there have been mixed reviews about the relevancy of "Internet Marketing" efforts. Some people use the internet exclusively for their campaigns, while others use a combination of things. It is imperative for business owners to invest in some form of advertising online.

You may be in the position that I once was; just wondering where to start. You can establish a presence online either organically or through a paid Google AdSense campaign. The organic way is time consuming and it is based on content marketing.

Many of our clients have different needs. We had one client that wanted to switch over to a WordPress platform. WordPress offers lower rates, but many people find it difficult to navigate. Businesses come to us in order to get the ultimate value along with a custom design. This particular client is a lifestyle blogger, and she hired our firm to help her transition her blog. She gave us the opportunity to redesign and rebrand her website for her. As I was working on transferring the data, I noticed how consistent she was on her blog. She posted content and social media posts in order to keep her audience engaged. She also gained a huge following over time as well.

In order to provide even more content, you may want to create a blog for your company. A blog will help you establish yourself as an industry expert. Next, you would need to determine what your keywords are in order to build content around them. If you follow these steps you can build a following organically.

A paid campaign requires a list of keywords that correlate with the brand and or service that you provide. Your keywords are words and phrases that your customer would use in order to find out about industry trends and/or your company and products. The overall objective of a pay-per-click campaign is to rank just as high as any competitor in your field.

Did Somebody Say Results:

People generally go into business to make money. We set goals in order to see results. Let me paint a picture for you:

Okay, so you have paid for your web design and your online store is up and running. You have a decent number of followers but you aren't making any money. You really don't understand what is going on because you have seemingly done everything that it takes. What should you do now? Well, as an Internet Marketing consultant I have learned through my own experiences that it is important for you to get an accurate analysis from time to time. This is something that should be done quarterly. An analysis will give you a clear picture as it relates to your marketing efforts. For example, if you see a decrease in sales between the first and second quarter, an analysis of your current marketing and sales practices can help bookmark pivotal moments in your yearly timeline. It can also give insight about annual trends within the industry. For example, if the holidays are approaching, you can begin to create a strategy ahead of time and see how it changes over time on an annual basis.

A proper analysis should tell you if your efforts are converting, website traffic sources, and the rate at which people are leaving your site with or without making purchases. All of this information is valuable, and it will help you determine how to go about creating a campaign. For example, if you are receiving most of your traffic through social media, it may be wise to create your campaign around that. Or, if the majority of your traffic comes from referrals, it may be wise create a campaign that caters to a referral based model. No matter the case, it is imperative to get a proper analysis. Receiving feedback about how your website is performing can save time and money.

I believe that entrepreneurship is a journey and a calling. I'm passionate about what I do. If I had any advice for you it would be to follow your passion. I love to see ideas go from obscurity to reality. It is exciting to see people live out their dreams. I do what I do in order to be of service and help others reach their fullest potential. Again, consistency, planning and focus are your friends. If you commit to these principles you will thrive. Planning changed my life. When I began to write things down, I was able to see the bigger picture. I also began to see my business go to the next level. Always remember that if you can think it, you can do it. Don't let anyone stop you from achieving your dreams and goals. It is totally possible for you to persevere and become successful in every facet of your industry. As long as you don't give up and you work hard, the sky is the limit.

ABOUT THE AUTHOR

Marketing strategist, Co-author and serial entrepreneur Christina Elkins-Thomas is committed to helping business owners maximize their potential. She helps entrepreneurs find marketing strategies that boost conversion rates and send sales through the roof. She attributes all of her victories to her personal relationship with God. She is a wife and the mother of two boys. In her free time, she enjoys listening to music and reading. She is the founder of Digital Marketing Mogul and Co-Founder of Elkins Family Enterprises.

Stay in touch with Christina:
www.digitalmarketingmogul.net
Instagram: @digitalmarketingmogul

CHAPTER FOUR

Mind(set) Over Matter

Lenise Williams

Entrepreneurship. Business. Self-employed. Those are just a few of the words that get me excited! I really love business. I would go as far as to say I am obsessed with business. I am always studying a person's business model, their success and using it all to learn. All day I am talking about business, studying business or doing business. It makes me smile to know that I have done what many dream of doing; I have built a business around my passion.

I am an intellectual property attorney and brand/business advisor. I help entrepreneurs build and grow their businesses and I also help them protect what they create through copyright and trademark protection. I get to help others build their entrepreneur dreams everyday. In addition, I am also the creative director and owner of Made Leather Company, a leather bag company that imports leather bags and goods from Morocco. I also host seminars and speak at events, both nationally and internationally, about entrepreneurship. I have authored several books about the journey of entrepreneurship including my best seller, *The 31 Day Guide to Building a Personal Brand.* I have a wide array of interests, but they all are tied back to business and entrepreneurship.

ENTREPRENEURSHIP: MY STORY, YOUR GUIDE

Many knew as children that they wanted to be a business owner. I did not always know that I wanted to be an entrepreneur. However, I did realize at an early age that maybe my thoughts and ideas were a little different than others. I was not the type of little girl that liked to play with dolls; I found it to be a waste of time. I enjoyed playing softball, but otherwise preferred to do something challenging and creative. My mom recognized my creative nature and registered me in art lessons. I enjoyed the art lessons, until one day I decided to quit. I quit because I wanted to be creative, but not have others tell me what to create. I wanted to create great artwork, but I wanted to create my vision, not someone else's. My mom did not understand my rationale, but she respected my wishes and withdrew me from the program. My mom just concluded that I was a different type of child as I also did not always play well with others; after awhile they just started to bore me. In high school when everyone was going to retail stores and fast food restaurants to get their first job, I was looking elsewhere. I was always looking for ways to work smart (and make more money) and not hard.

As a ten - year old I remember becoming annoyed with a friend because she did not want to be, what I now recognize as, my business partner. We both had beautiful dogs that were of the same pure breed. I had a male dog and she had a female. Ordinarily, puppies of this breed sold for $250 -$300 each. Once I realized how many puppies were in a typical litter, I thought breeding would be such a great (and profitable) idea. I could not understand why she did not want to do it. Even at ten years old it was puzzling that someone was not interested in making money. I suppose I could have been like the other ten year olds and sold lemonade or sold candy, but my eyes were always on something bigger. I have always thought big!

My ideas and my vision have always been larger than others could understand. Being a part of a middle-class family and experiencing the paycheck to paycheck lifestyle, of course to my family my thoughts and ideas were looked at as more like dreams as opposed to goals. I did not accept them as dreams and I worked hard to achieve the goals that others could not comprehend. I graduated from college, graduated from law school and became an attorney. It wasn't enough for me. I went on to own several successful businesses. Some were successful in other ways than monetary; some were a big monetary gain. Regardless of the gain or the loss, I learned something from all of my experiences. The biggest and most valuable lesson that I learned was that whatever I put my mind to, I can make it happen. With that principle as my foundation, I have achieved many feats.

Made Leather Company is my first product- based business. My other ventures were all primarily service-based. Nonetheless, many of the lessons and strategies learned in my service- based businesses have prepared me for my product-based venture. In this chapter, it is my goal to provide you with basic steps that you can take to find success in both a service or a product-based brand.

Success Mindset:

I have come to realize that regardless of the books you read, the seminars you attend or the businesses that you study, you will not achieve the level of success you may want if you don't believe that you can. Many people have notions about money that may have been ingrained in their brain as a child. For example, when I was a child and we would drive through a wealthy neighborhood my parents would look around and sometimes call the residents in the neighborhood "lucky". Although the words were never said, I felt as though we could never live in a home like those or be wealthy because; we just were not that lucky. This was a thought that crept from my subconscious in my late twenties and early thirties. I had to address these thoughts, for with them I would always have a fear or a doubt once I began making large amounts of money. I would always feel as though I wasn't one of those "lucky" people. I'd have thoughts like: "for sure this is a fluke; no one else will pay me this amount every again." Who was I to have great success and great wealth?? Having that fear or that limited mindset, which may or may not have been recognized at the time, will always keep a person stagnant. That is not the mindset of a successful entrepreneur.

If you work hard then you do deserve it all; you indeed are one of those "lucky" people! Don't allow your thoughts to get in the way of the life you envision for yourself. It is up to you to dig deep and determine not only what your limited beliefs are, but to also determine why you have them. It is much like having a reoccurring injury- you cannot continue to just medicate the injury. At some point, you need to find out why you continuously have the injury and then remedy the injury. It may take some time and it may even cause some tears, but it will be worth it. It took me a couple of years to get to the root of many of my mindset blocks. It pulled out some difficult memories and erupted so many tears. However, I am thankful for that part of the journey. In order to fix your outside circumstance, you must first fix what's within.

Social Media is Your Bestie:

Social media changed the way so many people do business, get news and even the way some date! Social media has definitely made doing business so much easier. Social media has made it possible to market a business, market an event and even market a person/persona. The platform is there, it is just up to entrepreneurs to take advantage of it.

Grow Your Tribe

Social Media is the best way to build a tribe of people that are crazy about you or what your company provides. Having good content, nice pictures and/or graphics and using relevant hashtags is the best way to build that audience. Not only do you have to provide the content and the graphics, but you have to do it consistently and in a manner that best suits the needs of your potential clients or customers. Doing just that for my legal and consulting business helped me go from zero clients to having to turn away clients. Of course, it did not happen overnight; it took at least a year or longer to effectively and consistently reach the right people and convert them into paying clients. However, I determined what my clients wanted to learn most about and provided it to them. I provided content in my area of expertise that I knew my potential clients wanted or needed through blog posts, great graphics to capture my ideal clients' attention and social media caption full of valuable information and through live streaming to demonstrate that I was not just full of knowledge, but also a real person with a personality.

Over time social media also helped my potential clients establish the trust that is essential for a service provider. For a service provider, consistently using social media allows time for followers that otherwise do not have the opportunity to meet you in person, to develop trust and feel as though they know you. This takes time. I have social media followers that contact me for a consultation that advise that they have been following me on social media for years; it is a process and consistency is key.

Hashtags Are a Big Deal

My biggest opportunity for Made Leather Company thus far came as the result of a hashtag. An NFL agent was searching for great weekender bag for the players that he represented. He searched #weekender bag and stumbled across my Instagram page. He liked what he saw, contacted me and we created a professional relationship and the rest is history! I was provided with the opportunity to provide bags for a number of NFL players. Although I gave them the bags at no cost, I still call it an opportunity, as the exposure it provided for my company has been priceless. The players loved their gifted bags! They were photographed with the bags and also gave me social media mentions to their millions of followers. The photographs provided credibility to my brand and the social media mentions resulted in sales. Further, the sales I received from other players that simply saw these guys with the amazing bags made it worth it. A simple hashtag created an opportunity that changed the trajectory of my business. Don't ever underestimate the power of a hashtag.

Give It Your Full Attention:

Yes, just like a child your business wants your time and your attention- lots of it. If you want your business to thrive you must nurture it. When I start on a new project I work on it or think about it all day every single day. I think about it when I wake-up and I am thinking about it when I go to sleep. I literally become obsessed with that project. I personally feel that obsession is the only way in which a person truly finds success. Obsession is typically looked upon as something that is unhealthy. However, finding the right thing to have an obsession is healthy and it can be classified as an individual's purpose for living.

It is believed that it takes roughly 10,000 hours of practice for someone to master a skill or a craft or to fully understand and have a grasp of a particular subject matter. Any unwavering interest, which allows one to easily obtain 10,000 hours of honing the skill or expertise, is exactly what obsession is. The great thing about being obsessed is that something has to happen. The more you push, the more there is movement – albeit large or small. The progress that results from obsession is inevitable. Just remember that there is no such thing as part time obsession or part time success; it is all or nothing.

I am addicted to business, obsessed with my success- I have found my passion. I read books, I attend seminars, I watch webinars and I watch how others move. Part of being obsessed is studying others for they have set the path; no need to reinvent the wheel. I do not watch much television. If I do it will likely be Shark Tank or The Prophet, or some other business based show. It is not intentional; I just do not have an interest in much else. Also, the people that I surround myself with are similar. I know many people, but I do not have many friends for it is hard to find people that understand my mindset and don't think my goals are crazy. I have found comfort in knowing that my obsession may be too much for others. Instead of trying to get people to understand, I just work on my businesses!

Get so focused on your goal that you don't even worry about the people around you that don't understand. Get so obsessed with your success that people step back and start to take notes from you. When you are obsessed and focused you can't become distracted. Distraction often results in failure.

Be Sure That Your Pricing is Right:

You are a business owner. Business owners start a business in order to make money, right? Of course you want a business the serves a need and has an impact, but I am sure that you also want it to make money. The problem is if you are nervous about talking about money or in setting your prices, you will lose! When I started my first law firm over ten years ago I just wanted someone, anyone to retain my services! I was a new mom and had little experience outside of law school. I had very little confidence in myself when comparing my skillset to a more seasoned attorney. That lack of confidence was evident in my pricing. For a while until I finally had enough, I had many clients and lots of work but my back account did not reflect that. I was working nonstop, but that was not reflected via my bank account. The problem? I was getting paid, but not getting paid what I was worth.

I later realized that it was more beneficial to have a few clients that were paying me the right amount of money as opposed to having lots of clients paying me less than I was worth. I learned to stop sacrificing so much of my time when I was not being compensated accordingly. That changed my life. After I had some experience under my belt, I was able to increase my fees and work with the right people. It took some time for this to really work. During the process, I had to turn down many clients that could not afford my rates, although I really needed the money. Instead of reducing my rates and sacrificing myself, I remained patient and eventually it paid off. Once the first "right" client came, it seemed as though that was all I was attracting thereafter. Remember, if you want to be underpaid and overworked, you can work for someone else.

I faced some of the same issues in my leather company. I learned from previous experience that I did not want the overhead of a brick and mortar location. The world is going online more and more in order to purchase things that they want. I opted to sell my products online; however, I still wanted a presence in retail locations. In order to achieve this, I had to set up wholesale pricing and pitch to retailers in order to have them carry my bags in their stores. Having wholesale pricing allows retailers to purchase products in bulk at a discounted price. The retailer in turn sells the items in their location for a higher price than they paid per item.

Initially, I decided that I would sell with wholesale pricing being about 35% less than my retail price online. When I began crunching numbers I realized that my margins were all wrong for a set up like that! I had to increase my retail price in order to set wholesale pricing that was profitable for me. I had to calculate my cost from the manufacturer, shipping from the manufacturer (remember, my manufacturer is in Morocco), cost for packaging, cost for assistant in Morocco to oversee operations, account for my time invested in ordering and also shipping the item to the retailer. Initially my pricing made cents; not sense! Taking all of the costs into consideration, I readjusted my retail pricing so that my wholesale pricing made dollars and not cents!

Pricing is vital to a service based and a product based business. Your business can become an absolute financial nightmare if this is not done properly. Don't be afraid to adjust it if you feel as though it is necessary. Adjust it until you finally get it right! The goal of entrepreneurship is freedom and the notion of being paid your worth. Remain patient and don't sell yourself short.

Grind Like You Are Broke

Everyday my goal is to work like I am poor! I look for leads, send follow-up emails, make follow-up phone calls, create content to keep my social media audience and email lists engaged as though I don't have any clients or customers. If I do not maintain this "hungry" mindset, I miss out on potential money in the future. Just because I have a good month I do not get comfortable. If I waste my time spending money and thinking about how great the previous month was, it is likely the following month will be disastrous. I don't ever get too comfortable.

As part of my "grind plan" I set an income goal. For each venture I determine how much I would like for it to generate annually. I then divide that number by twelve to determine my monthly goal. I go even further and divide the number by thirty in order to calculate my daily goal. Daily goals feel so much more attainable as opposed to looking at a large annual goal. When I break it down into a smaller goal I do not feel as discouraged.

After creating the daily goal, I can then devise a plan of how to make that particular amount of money in a day. For example, if the goal is hypothetically five hundred dollars per day, then I need to determine what products or services I need to sell in order to achieve the goal. If my products are one hundred dollars, then I need to be sure to sell five per day. If my products are twenty dollars each then I know that I need to sell twenty- five per day. I will set out to achieve this goal by calling potential clients/customers that I spoke with previously, posting on social media, sending out sales emails to my email list, etc. I will do whatever it takes to meet that daily goal as though my life depends on it. I suggest that you grind each and every single day as though you were on the verge of filing bankruptcy!

Don't Be Afraid to Reinvent Yourself

As a part of this entrepreneur journey you may get bored, people may get tired of you- who knows! The luxury that an entrepreneur has is that if they get bored or feel that their audience is no longer responding to them, they can do something different. As entrepreneurs, we can be as boring or an innovative as we'd like! It's fun!

The older/more mature we become, we realize that our interests and possibly our priorities change. Of course as we grow as individuals, our business must change as well. Just as some "outgrow" their 9-5 job, the same can happen in a business. At this point in my life, I am not afraid to do something outside of the box nor am I afraid to do something in a totally different industry. If something interests me, it is a viable idea and I have the time to commit to it, I pursue it.

Marketing strategies change, other people's interests change, everything changes- you cannot be afraid to change with it. Reinventing yourself may be the key to your ongoing happiness. Reinvention should not be used as a way to run away from something else, yet as a tool to help you live out your passion. And yes, despite what you have heard, it is possible to have more than one passion!

In my years of consulting with business owners on how to get their brands up and running, I too got the itch to start something new. I enjoy helping others with their business, but I started to miss having my own. Yes, my legal and consulting business was my own, but I wanted more! This is mostly because I am the type of person that gets bored with monotony; I want something different. I may possibly have undiagnosed ADHD! When things get stagnant or monotonous, I sometimes add something to my life! This time I added Made Leather! It broke up the monotony, it was interesting and it made dollars. It was perfect for me.

Family Lawyer, Criminal Lawyer, turned serial entrepreneur and business consultant. I have had an interesting fifteen-year journey of reinvention and I am loving every minute of it!

In closing, there are no two entrepreneurial stories that are exactly the same. There are no two businesses in the same industry with the same start-up story. Every single business has a different set of circumstances. Every entrepreneur has experiences which shape them and the decisions that they make. Some of the things that work for me may not work for someone else and vice versa. What I do know is that with a success mindset, execution, a bit of obsession, a social media strategy, proper pricing and lots of grind, your story is destined to have a happy ending.

ABOUT THE AUTHOR

Lenise Williams is an advocate for entrepreneurship. Not only is she an advocate, she is also an Intellectual Property Attorney and Business Strategist. She works with existing businesses to develop more profitable brands and assure that a brand's intellectual property (trademark, copyright, patent) is protected. Although she has an extensive list of training and degrees, her expertise is also from personal experiences as a serial entrepreneur owning and operating multiple businesses for nearly 15 years.

In order to fulfill her goal to encourage entrepreneurship and women in leadership positions, Lenise travels hosting seminars and public speaking. Lenise has spoken to small groups of national and international college students to gracing international stages such as the United Nations 2016 Conference in Marrakech, Morocco and Hive Global Leaders Program in Africa. In addition, Lenise has worked with large companies such as Home Depot and Zaxby's Chicken Franchise to companies with only member.

Lenise is also the founder of several businesses, including Made Leather Company. Additionally, Lenise is the author of the books "31 Day Guide to Building a Personal Brand", "She Conquered" and "Business, Babies, Balance: Tales of Mompreneurs". Lenise uses her platform and her books as a means to help others find the freedom she has found through entrepreneurship.

Lenise is also the mother of two boys, Marcus age 12 and Evan age 10. She and her family reside in Atlanta, Georgia.

Stay in touch with Lenise:
www.LeniseWilliams.com
www.MadeLeatherCo.com
Instagram: @mompreneur_esq
Facebook: @momprenueresq

CHAPTER FIVE
For The Love of Resale:
It's How You "Rock" It
Osnita L. Norman

My Story:

I am Osnita L. Norman, owner of Pure Essence Resale Boutique, LLC located in Warren, Michigan. I knew deep down inside I wanted to be an astute business woman carrying a beautiful briefcase. My career had always been in Corporate America, but I wanted something different. I always wanted to own a resale shop, but had no clue of how to put my dream in motion.

My life changed when I had to take a semester off from school due to a life-changing event. During that semester off, just to keep my brain active, I signed up to receive an Entrepreneurial Certificate in a Continued Education program at Macomb Community College. Enrolling in that program changed my life and my thought process on who and what I wanted to become. I was set on starting the resale business; however, I knew I had to finish school and first obtain my degree. Once I completed my Bachelors of Science Degree in 2013 from Central Michigan University, my next mission was to get the Resale Boutique off the ground and running.

It only made sense for me to enter the fashion industry! When I think of where my love and passion for fashion was established, I have to reach back to my childhood. I would say my love for fashion and my style came from my father, mother and sisters. My father was a stylish Pastor with suits from the men's store Cousin's, and big block gators from the shoe store City Slickers, located in Michigan. I was always embarrassed by his attire of dress pants, shirt, and shoes every day. I later realized that my dad had an undeniable style!

My dad's style rubbed off on my sisters too! I was intrigued with my sisters and the way they would put outfits together to step out to a social event, or church etc. In my mind, all I could imagine was becoming a grown woman being dressed fancy, stylish and appealing like my sisters.

At an early age my mom always taught us quality over quantity. She did not believe in wasting money on cheap clothing. Her motto is "You get what you pay for." My mom would bring home bags of clothing from her employer with all kind of quality designer clothing. I would select items that caught my eye. I created my own panache from clothes considered as rummaged clothing. It was not mandatory for me to wear rummaged clothing; it was by choice as I enjoyed being different from others. I never wanted to look trendy like everyone else. As a teenager I didn't see that I was creating my own style with modern fashionable pieces. I just wanted to look crisp and classy.

Growing up, my Saturday mornings were the best because my mom and I would go to estate sales and garage sales in various neighborhoods looking for fantastic deals on odds and ends. I would always find nice designer items in good to excellent condition. I loved to show it all off, just to rave about the price I paid for it. The amusing part was that no one ever believed me! I remember purchasing a beautiful vintage Louis Vuitton Monogram Cartouchiere shoulder bag for which I paid five dollars. Currently today this bag resales for $345.00. Over time I have come across so many other great finds. The beauty in resale shopping is finding the best for less.

Currently, the vast majority of my wardrobe consists of 70% resale items. Over time I have learned to build my wardrobe with key pieces, especially the basic black go-to items: blazer, dress, pants and skirt. You always want to ensure that those pieces are of nice quality because you can always put together a stylish ensemble with key pieces. My style was very basic, until I began to receive conversational fashionable gifts that took me out of my comfort zone. A conversational piece is an item that allows you to engage in conversation about it based on a person admiring your style. I consider my style as crazy, sexy and cool. My outfit choice merely depends on my mood. I don't dress for "the" occasion; I'm dressed for any occasion.

I have really developed a love for resale fashion. What I love about resale fashion is that you can express yourself in a way that no one else can. Whether it's trendy, classic or vintage it's all about your creativity. The average person does not know there is a difference between fashion and style. Fashion is defined as a popular trend that is current during a particular time among a particular group of people. Style is, "unique to each person". Each person creates his or her own style through their own choice of clothing, shoes and accessories. There are many people in the world that do not believe in fashion, but believe in style because they wear what makes them smile. In my opinion resale fashion is like listening to music. You dance to music the way you hear the beat, so you style yourself according to a beat that calms you.

My Industry:

The average person once thought that a resale business is mainly for trash that no one wants. I look at resale as an industry of treasure. Treasure is defined as thing(s) that are valued for its rarity, valued highly, apple of one's eye or something you hold dear to your heart. What was old to another is a treasure to you. I hold resale treasures to my heart because when shopping I look for items that I didn't want to pay top dollar for and items that are different. Resale items to me are conversational pieces because I always receive the most compliments on items that were gifted to me or those that I paid less than retail price for.

The resale market has changed tremendously, as the demand to get high-end designer item(s) for a fraction of the cost has risen. Being the owner of Pure Essence has given me the chance to share knowledge and provide hands on expertise of the resale industry experience to my clients. According to Thredup.com, apparel resale, both offline and online, make up an $18 billion-dollar industry in thrifting and is expected to increase by 2021. Many consumers today, want more merchandise for their buck. High-income shoppers that earn a six to seven figure income are 35% more likely to buy resale than low-income shoppers. (thredup.com)

The resale industry has grown so much, that there is a national organization. NARTS, short for The National Association of Resale Professionals, provides educational and professional development for future and current owners of resale stores. NARTS was established in 1984 with 5 members and now the association currently has over 1,000 members.

Many understand the industry, but there are others do not. More often than not I've had consumers walk past my vendor table and turn their head because my sign states "resale" just to stop at another table and purchase an item that may not be of quality, but is considered "new" merchandise. What I have figured out is that all clothing that we purchase from traditional retail stores are also resale item(s). You may ask how? Your favorite shoes, dress, pants and top has been tried on by several persons, or unknown to you it was purchased and returned to the selling floor. The difference with resale is that you are being told upon receipt that the item you are purchasing is new with tags, new without tag, or gently worn. Most shoppers don't understand that concept.

There are many people whom indulge in resale, but are too ashamed to flaunt it. I call them silent resale shoppers. Some of my social media engagers will ask me directly under my post, and I have some will inbox me inquiring on a posted item. Either way works for me. If you are silent or vocal when it comes to resale shopping it is totally up to you. Being able to successfully shop resale and retail is considered having options. When you work hard you should play the way you want and if resale shopping is it then allow that to be your glee. I never care what anyone else thinks of my fashion choices because people will find error in your fashion because they don't have the fashionista or fashionmista key to the closet. The purpose is to stand out not blend in; with style, you depict your own fashion.

May 28, 2017, I had the opportunity to change other's perspective of the resale industry. I was able to promote resale as it ripped the runway with Walk Fashion Show. This was the experience of a lifetime as I had never physically been in a national Fashion Show. I was incredibly nervous prior to the show, hoping all the models showed up and their outfits would grab the attention of the crowd. I was anxious to see how the audience would respond to resale products on the runway. I took pride in my presentations; therefore, I presented my set as if this was my last chance. I gave this opportunity my all and it displayed itself from the many astounding comments and accolades I received during and after the show. At the end of the evening I was able to view the video and was amazed at the cameras flashing, people clapping and my family in the crowd screaming loud and proud. Walking the runway was an exciting and wonderful rush. My overall experience will forever play in my head because I provided the crowd with a different perspective of resale fashion. I have proven that resale is fashion too; it's just styled to the liking of the individual wearing it.

My Journey:

Once I decided to start my online resale business, I had the items and the knowledge, but no name for the business. I jotted down about 25 names and not one stood out. I wanted a name that identified with me and my dreams. I also wanted a name that would be inclusive to all genders. Therefore, the name had to be eloquent and captivating to all.

I am the youngest of five amongst my siblings so I sought their expertise and began asking each of them for assistance. Each sibling listened and provided their feedback. It was not until my older brother stated to me: "select a name with meaning and class, like the Essence Magazine; one word describes it all!" then it all came together. I put some thought to the word "meaning", and began researching words and thinking of names that had a describable meaning. I had registered my business name, received my Tax ID number (EIN).

February 2013 Pure Essence Resale Boutique, LLC was established and the journey began. On my twenty-fifth birthday, I received my first sewing machine. This special gift opened my eyes to the art of sewing. I enrolled and completed a few classes to learn the basics of sewing. I began going to the fabric store and buying tons of fabric and patterns only to realize that sewing with a guided pattern did not work out well for me. Pre-made patterns have too many tedious steps for that perfect finish. I preferred creating my own fashionable creations. My first non-pattern creation was a denim purse that I made from an old pair of jeans. Being introduced to sewing brought out my creativity and it allowed me to look deeper into the art of fashion, material, apparel and designers. Anyone can love clothing, but knowing your upscale clothing designers makes the art of resale shopping an even better experience. This knowledge allows a reseller to be a better consumer, as they can identify designer names and pricing. They are able to recognize the better brands and have the ability to shop them for less.

Once Pure Essence Resale Boutique was ready to make its debut there were many people whom had never heard of an online resale boutique. They were anxious to see what I had to offer. Because my presence at the time was strictly online, my goal was for the website presentation to be very professional. To achieve that goal, I ensured that all items to be sold on the website were professionally photographed. I did not want inconsistency with the clarity of pictured items on the site. I wanted viewers to know that I took pride in my website presentation. Further, I also took the time to perfect my style and appearance that when potential clients and business associates connected with me they would know that I meant business. Online and offline presentation is everything as some potential customers give you one chance to make that lasting impression.

I also made sure that I always had nice quality items on myself as I am a reflection of my business. I always tell existing and potential clients that I would not offer clothing, shoes or accessories to anyone in a condition that I would not purchase for myself. Therefore, I ensure that I offer nothing but the best in resale. Being particular has paid off as each client that I have serviced has been happy with his or her purchases from Pure Essence and they continue to return along with their friends and family.

Funding:

I believe in achieving goals to perfection. I knew the vision that I had would not be brought to fruition for free, but I needed to start somewhere. I also knew that I did not want to take out a loan. Knowing that I would be opening my resale shop I began to collect clothing to begin fulfilling my dream, but it was not enough. I needed funds. What was I to do? I continued to work to figure out how I was going to begin this journey with minimal funds. I continued thinking, searching and planning. During my thought process, I had begun researching successful icons in the fashion industry, reading books and watching videos just to see what I could find.

ENTREPRENEURSHIP: MY STORY, YOUR GUIDE

I remember hearing an industry influencer state that one should market and sell products where the overhead is low. That includes shared workspace or Flea Market, etc. That didn't sound like a bad idea. There was a Flea Market not far from my home where I could set up. I contacted Gibraltar Trade Center in Mt. Clemens, Michigan and was provided information on how to get started. I paid $12.00 for a spot on a Friday and was up and running on Saturday. This was just the beginning of my journey. I continued to rent tables at Gibraltar during their Garage Sale Extravaganza's and their Mom to Mom sales to keep the money flowing in order to fund my bigger vision. Gibraltar Trade Center allowed me to showcase Pure Essence items and show people a more upscale side of resale.

At the time, my business was strictly online; I would continuously do vendor events to fund, network, educate myself and showcase my items. My first vendor event gave me the courage to network and present my brand. I was confident in what I had to offer and my presentation was capturing, but I was nervous. However, that experience provided me with continued confidence I am able to display today. What I learned in supporting pop-up shops and vendor events was that every event was not for my brand. As a nascent entrepreneur, I just wanted to be a part of an event. I learned quickly "if it don't make dollars, it don't make sense!" I realized that I had to be more selective about the events for which I chose to be a part of for my brand. You have to walk away from each event feeling accomplished. You always want to make lots of money, but you also want to gain clients. I have invested plenty of my own funds into the business not expecting anything in return. Seeing a client walk away excited because of a product that I had to offer is an accomplishment for me.

Keep your business and your personal funds separate when you are trying to build your business. You can see your profits and losses easier. If you are not good at handling funds hire an accountant to do the job, as you want to be able to control your spending.

Why Entrepreneurship?

I am a mother, daughter, niece and aunt who takes this entrepreneurial journey serious because I want to be an influencer. I became an entrepreneur because I wanted to make a difference, as I have a testimony about building self-confidence through fashion. That is still my desire; however, my motivation has also become my son and my second generation of nieces and nephews. I am helping to build their confidence by providing them options to know that they can be their own boss.

As I evolved from dreaming to doing I introduced my son, Jayson II, to the entrepreneurial journey also. Each time I would vendor at events I would take him with me. In the beginning, he only wanted to roam around and shop. One day he approached me about purchasing him an expensive video game. He had witnessed me sell his clothing at local Mom to Mom sales, and he had even brought a few toys to sell also, but he had no goal. Jayson, II had been saving his money but still needed eighty dollars to make his purchase. By him wanting this game it allowed me to help him change his thought process. I advised him that he could make his own money and I explained to him that if he sold his old clothing, and toys in his closet he could make the additional money to purchase the game. I decided to purchase a table solely for him to sell his items that he selected for resale: clothing, shoes and toys. All the profit was going in his pocket. Once we ended the day he had made his eighty dollars. He was very excited and felt very accomplished. He began to have a drive and passion for making money.

My role as a mother at that moment was to teach him how it feels to want something and have the means and the drive to earn it. I continue to encourage him to find his niche on what he wants to do along with teaching how to build his own wealth by thinking and saving. Currently, he works with me and I continue to educate him on entrepreneurship.

Being an entrepreneur does not come with instructions because each person that steps into this journey does so for different reasons. You have many people who want to become an entrepreneur because they never want to punch someone else's time clock and some that do it because they do not have any other choice. Being your own boss is great, but most forget the grind and grit it takes to succeed, fail and stay motivated while you are trying to achieve greatness. I'm sure you have read in books or heard speakers say that being an entrepreneur is not easy. The journey can be fun in the end when everything works out the way you envisioned; however, I've had my moments when I wanted to give up. To keep myself motivated I have to pull out my journal and read my thoughts from a place where I once was. Reading old thoughts encourages me to keep pushing to succeed.

ENTREPRENEURSHIP: MY STORY, YOUR GUIDE

You should keep a journal, or notebook handy to write down your thoughts and plans. (Ex. People you want to network with, view a website, an article, book to buy etc.) Writing frees up your mind. If you don't write it down within seconds, you will forget your great idea or task. Once you write it down and review then you can add to your strategy later.

I am also encouraged to keep going when I help women exude confidence that they didn't know they had. As a boutique owner, you always want to show a person that no matter their body size that they can always turn heads. My responsibility is to help women and men build their confidence level to finally know and feel like they can turn heads. Many people ask me about my selection of clothing, not understanding how I can mix colors, patterns, labels and it all looks so well put together. It took time for me to feel more confident and achieve my goal. I show women how I do it and advise women to embrace you and don't be afraid to wear something different. Add color, mix patterns, and materials, it's ok to be different. How much you spend is not the factor, it's your presentation that is important. No one knows how much you spent but you! Rock your style!

As women, we can be our own worst critics by being concerned of what others think. I entered into this world of fashion to teach women how to embrace themselves no matter what shape or size they are. Be the best you that you can be! Flaunt your style, shape and size because you might give another person confidence that they never thought they had. I've had the privilege to do personal shopping and styling for women that just don't know how to make an outfit pop. You have one chance to "wow" the room! Make it worth your while. As a woman that has had life experiences you should be able to be bold and express the best you that allows you to build inner confidence and show it on the outside.

Testimonial: Osnita has always has a sense of fashion, it seems she was born with this gift. I thought I had it all figured out until I was to attend a Prom for Mom event in 2016. I had waited until the day of to prepare my outfit, but what I put together was not making me smile. I called Osnita in a panic about what to wear. She went asked me a few questions, I sent a few pictures and she was able to confidently assist me. I was shocked because she did this all through pictures and conversation. I was determined to make this event because I had missed my own Senior Prom.

Needless to say, I entered the Prom Event with confidence, flair and compliments. —Beverly

Testimonial: *Shopping with Pure Essence is always a pleasure. I know that I will find pieces that are cute, trendy and compliments my style for a reasonable price! -Janel*

Marketing Tips:

Marketing your brand has to be the most challenging part of entrepreneurship especially if you want to grow your brand successfully. Marketing is evolving minute-by-minute, day-by-day. As an entrepreneur you have to step out of your comfort zone. You have to stay abreast as to the changing market. I ensure that I continuously collect emails, phone numbers, and all social media sites from potential clients that Pure Essence encounters. I always keep my business cards along with my discount flyers available at all times when I am out and about as you never know who will be your next potential client.

You always want to make sure that your marketing content is consistent from your business cards, flyers, signs, etc. Consistency is what clients and potential clients, and persons that are looking to build partnerships through networking and events look for. Part of that consistency includes staying in contact with your potential and existing clients and keeping them engaged. Each time I have an event I ensure that I provide my clients with something to take home that will always allow them to remember Pure Essence and the experience they had.

I have learned to create experiences for my clients by implemented a few gestures. Here are a few that you can use:

-Always follow up with a Thank you card or email after engaging with clients.

-Listen and get to know your clients' favorite item, color etc.

Ex: If they love purses send that "Just in" email or text advising. You can also add discounts, etc.

-You have to make your clients feel special.

Social Media:

Social media is key to any flourishing business. Being able to go live and engage with friends and followers is a great tool to use, as clients and potential clients get to engage with you on a more personal level which allow them to feel they know you and your brand better. Instagram is great to attract followers and clients especially with the hash tags. Just think of how you use the search engine on Google. Potential clients that are looking for a service or product search the same way on Instagram. I suggest searching hashtags that is related to your business that can draw potential clients to your page. I have networked with people through Instagram which allowed me to build business relationships.

Additionally, you have to be consistent with posting your items on all of your social media sites. For example, whatever I post on Facebook I post on Instagram for consistency, because clients and potential clients may not all be on every social media site. You never want them to feel left out. Know your client! I will post a repeat item until it sells. Also, I will use the same picture with different content depending on how that item coincides for the day, holiday or an event that may be taking place. You don't have to post or email every day to be consistent, you just have to select consistent days that work for your schedule. As your followers will begin to track your trend and know when you will engage with them. When you receive a comment, you should always respond within 24 to 48 hours to positive comments so the follower(s) feel that you enjoy connecting with your audience.

Create Events:

Create events that are specific to your brand. Twice yearly I host a Sip, Shop and Consign event to showcase my Fall/Winter and Spring/Summer Fashions for the seasons. Being consistent allows my friends, family, clients and followers to stay abreast as to the coming events. I plan the events the same month and weekend for the upcoming seasons. In marketing consistency is key!

I am enjoying the entrepreneurial journey, as it has allowed me to grow. Being able to make a difference in a person's life is monumental. Each time I think of how much success I have gained, I smile because I was able to make my dream a reality. My main goal is and will continue to be to make a difference in a person's life whether it be man, woman, boy or girl; I want to influence. I want to be an inspiration to someone who felt they couldn't do it. I want to motivate the person who was on the verge of giving up because life got in the middle of the plan and purpose that was meant for their life. Giving up is easy, but pursuing a dream and achieving goals that you are passionate about is hard.

I've had my moments where I felt wretched, but I would always end up talking to someone who needed my words for inspiration and motivation. I would share my story and through sharing, it motivated me to continue to pursue my passion. I want to leave a legacy for my son Jayson, II to recognize that his mom built a business from scratch. My son loves Lego's and he is always looking to add to his collection. He says, "Building with Legos is going to help me become an Engineer." He is great at building, so I continue to encourage and help him to build toward his goal. Some may say, "It's just Legos". However, Legos come with instructions and if not built properly you end up with random pieces that you have to figure out how to rebuild. In the end, it's like being an entrepreneur you have to learn how to build your business and plan in a way that creatively works for you. For your vision, you don't have to follow the trend or the same rules as everyone else. You use the research and knowledge learned and apply it your way.

After reading this chapter I hope I have inspired, motivated and added determination for you to just put your mind to it and just do it! There is no time like now! Life will get in the way as obstacles come in to add another paragraph to your story. You don't want to live with regrets. Perfect what you can and everything else will fall into place. You want to be able to say I learned, I tried, and I was successful.

It's not where you buy it, it's how you "Rock" it!

ABOUT THE AUTHOR

Osnita was born and raised on the eastside of Detroit, Michigan. She is the youngest of five children. She has a Bachelors of Science Degree from Central Michigan University. She loves fashion, music, dancing, and making people laugh. Entrepreneurship has allowed her to blossom and step out of her comfort zone.

"Osnita, I look at you as a fashion guru. I have always admired how you think outside the box or your comfort zone to help and encourage others to strive to be different when dressing for an occasion. Being able to help family, friends and clients create an image to express themselves with confidence and pride owning their style. May God continue to bless your gift in the fashion industry to share your skills with the world." -Jayson E. Mensah

Stay in touch with Osnita:
website: www.pureessenceresale.com
Instagram: @pure_essence_resale
Facebook: @pure.essence.resale

CHAPTER SIX

I TRUSTED MY GUT

Mindy P. Hobley

ENTREPRENEURSHIP: MY STORY, YOUR GUIDE

The Beginning:

Where I grew up there was lots of grass to watch grow, cows to feed and time to daydream. I used to complain to my parents about how bored I was, and this is because the World Book Encyclopedia was not enough for this young girl's imagination.

I, alongside my two younger brothers, grew up in the very small, very rural, river parish of Pointe Coupee in southern Louisiana in a tiny town called Glynn, with my wonderful parents. We call it "the country," and they say, "If you blink your eyes while passing it, you will miss it." As a young girl, I can remember walking up my parent's long, graveled driveway without shoes [ouch], and daydreaming about my future. I dreamed of living the higher life; a life with regular massages and manicures and pedicures. A life where I could purchase anything that I wished.

You see, I grew up with parents who worked in the education system and got paid once per month with my dad working as a carpenter on weekends to make ends meet. We were rich in family and culture and not so much in earthly possessions. At the very top of each month, they would buy groceries at a big box store and bring home food for the entire month. This was a high time for my two brothers and I as we helped them put the groceries away and celebrated with dancing at the excitement of big gallons of ice cream, boxes of Lil Debbie cakes and bags of fresh fruit for snacking after school. I still remember that at the end of every month, we would create stuff for snacking like tomato sandwiches and melted cheese on top of anything to make it taste good.

I am not very sure of the point when I made a conscious decision to become an entrepreneur. I can recall being told when I was about 5 years old, as my mom rolled into a parking lot of a grocery store, that I should not ask for anything in the store because we didn't have the money for anything extra. I believe that from the words" NO" and the lack of extra, I started very early to dream of a life where I could do or have anything I dreamed. Dreaming was free, and I did lots of it. I have always been a dreamer and very visual, and now I realize this is where it all began. It was the spark of a thought, a glimpse of a vision, or an idea of a feeling I wished to have.

I am not sure how or why, but something deep inside of me, I will call it "my gut," or you may call it God, told me that I could have whatever I wanted in my life. My friends tell me that I see life through rose colored glasses and that may very well be true; but I trust my gut and it keeps me positive, excited and energetic.

I can recall when I started to dream and play with the idea of owning my own salon and came to the conclusion that I was up for the challenge. I was to make the lives of multicultural people, like myself, easier. I wanted to figure out, what makes pretty hair go and how I could do it.

I am a light-skinned black woman of creole culture. If anyone knows anything about multicultural people, we have up to two to four different textures of hair on one head. It was a real problem for me when I got to high school. Lots of my friends were straight, smooth haired people and it was loud and clear that I was different when we were cheering at football games. At the games, their hair was smooth, straight and would lay flat and my hair would end up being a horrible, embarrassing frizz bomb. One time it was so bad, I went to the ladies' bathroom and stuck my head under the faucet and dowsed my hair in water to calm it from being a frizzy mess.

These feelings of hair problems followed me as I grew up because we didn't have extra money for me to visit a beauty salon. The closest I came to a hair salon most of the time was in my mom's kitchen. We permed it, ironed it, cut it, rolled it and hoped for the best. Each time I wished upon the answer to a lifelong question …" why does it do what it does and how can I make it better? " This became my mantra and led to my career in the beauty industry.

Having unruly, thick, frizzy, curly hair was always an issue for me even as an adult. I started to imagine that bringing a curly hair salon that gives relief and solves the problem for so many people dealing with the timely and challenging chore of doing their own hair.

When my parents asked me what I wanted to do after high school I knew immediately. As a matter of fact, at about the age of 15, I knew exactly what I wanted to do. I wanted to enroll in a great beauty school in New Orleans and figure this hair thing out.

I was always a kid to ask why and this new beauty school experience was the answer. I enrolled in John Jay beauty school in 1986 and devoured every moment. I finished and began my journey in the New Orleans area with beauty and hair services. I even entered a few hair shows and placed in all of them. What I was starting to realize was "whatever I would put my mind to, comes to life."

Approximately 18 years later, I was working on a client creating pretty smooth curls, when I let my mind wander and the thoughts of owning my own salon started to play. Excitement and wonder came across my being and the word "ringletts" popped in my head. I let it roll off my tongue, thought about it a moment and told my co-worker about the name. Just that fast "my gut" said yes! "Ringletts with two t's will be my new salon name!"

I can remember when I talked to my brother, Joe, about my new salon idea. He told me to make a proposal for him to see how serious I was. Of course, I went right to work to sort out what was in my head and put it all on paper. I crunched numbers and figured out logistics for a location and employees, furniture, etc. I studied business plans and gave him my best version of a proposal. After reviewing the proposal and seeing how passionate I was about my plan to be in business for myself, he believed in me enough to max his personal credit card and loan me $15,000 to finance my dream.

This was it! It was going to really happen, and I had the tenacity, true grit and desire to stretch every dollar to make this dream happen. My mom taught me that if you put things together with class and taste rather than just spending a lot of money, you come out ahead.

I took that money, which was about $10,000 less than what I really needed to start, and got to work. My dad helped build my cabinets for storage. I price shopped and cut corners and stretched dollars. I painted walls myself, and with the help of friends and family, Ringletts got all the way together.

By April 2005, I was the 100% owner of my new baby, and she was called Ringletts. With mostly second-hand furniture and equipment and design on a dime, I did it. Ringletts was a hit! It was located on the affluent lakefront marina, in New Orleans, Louisiana where all the boats and yachts were parked. It was perfect. I had a 10-chair salon, and it was a living and breathing entity. I owe it to my brother for believing in me and the support I received from my parents, other family members and friends.

Fortunately, I knew how to stretch a dollar!! I can recall when I first learned to stretch a dollar in 6th or 7th grade. At that time Nike had just come out with their first sneaker. It was all the rage. All the kids were rocking that Nike check on the side of their shoe. I came home and shared with my mom about the cool Nike sneakers everyone was wearing; but as I figured that Nike price tag was out of the budget. One Saturday after cleaning up the house my mom and I went to our favorite store, K-mart.

I went to check out the shoe department as I always did and low and behold, they had a cool knock off of that exact same Nike sneaker. It was the same color and the same style that the kids at school wore. Excitedly, I showed it to my mom and she told me she could get them. I was so happy! They were white with a blue check on the side. They looked exactly like the Nike sneakers I so adored, but it had an extra strip on the check; that was the only difference.

I went to school and in my mind, I was winning because I was just as stylish and in fashion as all the Nike wearers, with the same look and flavor. What I learned is that I didn't have to spend lots of money on anything to look great, that I could stay in my budget and still look phenomenal. I implemented that mindset into my salon.

Trials and Tribulations:

It feels as if it were yesterday. I can recall on a Saturday morning, just five months after launching Ringletts, that there was talk of a hurricane. A voluntary evacuation was issued and I decided to leave early that day. I remember advising my employees to pick up all equipment from the lower areas and place them up high so that if flood happens, we would not lose anything. I recall the salon was full of people that day. More people were calling that day because everyone needed their hair done before evacuating the city.

I can also recall talking to my brother, and not wanting to leave New Orleans for this hurricane. He told me if the hurricane is as big as they say it will be, there will be dead bodies floating in the water. Needless to say, after getting a visual of that image in my head, I fled my city and the business that I loved at 3 am that next morning. I believed that I would return home in a few days.

On August 29, 2005, Hurricane Katrina hit New Orleans and caused the levee system to break at the very area my Ringletts Salon was located. Tears and feelings of hopelessness consumed me as I watched my city and my business that I so loved, wash away within 24 hours. There was sadness, despair, confusion all around. There was nothing I could do but pray and cry.

Should I move to another city?

Was it going to be L.A. or Dallas?

How would I raise my daughter?

Anxiety set in and I didn't know what I was going to do.

I went to lay down and take a nap because I was tired and stressed; naps always help to clear my mind and recharge my soul. When I woke up my phone rang. I had a call from a dear client telling me that she had lost everything, but she needed her hair done....

What! They still needed me??!!!

Then I received another phone call, another client looking for me, "Where are you Mindy, I need you."

What!! I can make a difference??!!!

What! I can do something about my situation!

My mind started to turn; I had this burst of energy! I had to figure this out. I started looking in the newspaper for places to work, but by now I was having lots of clients calling me to service them immediately. I took a shot in the dark and asked my parents if I could set up shop in the garage. They didn't flinch and immediately told me yes. I found a hair chair, shampoo bowl, mirror, and a couple of dryers. My dad installed all of the equipment in their garage and my business went from Ringletts New Orleans (Lakefront Marina) to Ringletts, Glynn (in my parent's garage) within one week.

People came from all over to visit the garage. They were displaced all over the country, and they all made pit stops to get their hair done as they traveled to and fro. I realize now that I offered them something familiar in a world where they had lost everything. There was laughter and tears, advice and therapy sessions. There was comfort given in that garage. There were young, old, affluent and common folks that came to the garage. We all comforted each other because we were all one, grounded to the same level by Hurricane Katrina.

One morning as I was cranking heads out in the garage, my dad saw how many cars were parked outside in the driveway. He asked me, "What are you doing to those people, Mindy?" I chuckled, "Just their hair dad". I guess he had never seen his driveway look like a parking lot. For four months, I worked in the garage servicing locals and New Orleans travelers. That period of time showed me that I had a strong calling to return to New Orleans and reopen Ringletts.

I did just that. When I moved back to New Orleans I was able to work at my sister-in-law's salon in the outskirts of New Orleans. With $4000, even less of a shoestring budget than the first Ringletts, I launched her again. I reopened in September 2006 in a small commercial shotgun house that I rented on Canal Street in New Orleans. It was only big enough for four chairs, but it was all I could afford. Being that I did not have flood insurance at the first location, I had to start from the ground up again while still paying my brother back the original loan. I rolled up my sleeves, dug deep and focused on my craft one day at a time. Reveling in the idea that I was back in my city that I loved so much... and all was well.

I paid my brother back within a year and by 2008 I expanded to a twelve- chair flagship salon. Additionally, I gained a following of hundreds of clients and became a sought-after salon to work in due to my belief system of teaching and helping other stylists reach their goals.

My system to success was simple: to have a great salon I needed great stylists. I learned that the only way to get that was to create them from scratch. I hired stylists straight from beauty school and I taught them my tricks of the trade, including people skills. We stayed on top of the latest industry techniques and technology. I taught a lesson each day; there was a sisterhood, a beautiful flow of success and happiness. I witnessed my stylists go from a Junior stylist position to buying houses and cars.

I single-handedly took people straight from beauty school and created careers for them. Through positive mentoring, I helped them perfect their craft and I fed them clients so that they could make a living. By the summer of 2014, Ringletts was a fully occupied salon; we were very busy and profiting respectively.

Put in the Work Then Trust:

I got a phone call from a very close relative, and she told me that she needed to see me in person to tell me something she heard. I made time for the meeting and what she told me made my heart drop to my foot. She informed me that a few of my stylists were in the works of opening their own salon a few blocks away. She notified me that they had already began construction on their new salon. It felt as though the room got smaller and my breath got choppy. I couldn't see; I was in a state of shock. Nothing prepared me for this. I did everything I could to make each stylist happy and busy.

When you grow your stylists from a beginner's level, there is a risk that you will lose them eventually. However, I did not expect for this to happen in secret, right under my nose. I was now aware of backstabbing conversations and energies held in my business. I was really disturbed that they had the balls to use my business as a model for their new salon. This happened while they were working everyday in my establishment without one word, an ounce of respect, appreciation, nor any honesty. I felt betrayed. In addition to feeling betrayed, I was also fearful that I would lose my business once again.

It happened. One by one my stylists took flight. It lingered on for days and slowly I came to realize that I had experienced a "walkout." The deceit, disloyalty and sheer lack of regard for me after I single-handedly showed them the way to success. It caused pain that was almost unbearable. I believe that Hurricane Katrina was a walk in the park compared to this.

By December 2014, all of the stylists had walked out. I lost 95% of my employees and my client base was down by 90%. I believed I was finished and it was indeed one of the lowest moments of my life.

How could I ever come back?

Why didn't they tell me?

Why hurt me when all I ever did was help, teach and mentor?

How could I ever resurrect Ringletts this time?

Where were all the clients?

How would I quickly get new stylists that were good enough?

At my lowest point, I wished death and desperation on each and every person that had anything to do with the walkout. Everyone close to me told me not to give up. I heard them, but I didn't see how I could do that. In my head, I was doomed; but God had a different plan.

I managed to peel myself off my couch and put away the razor blade that I was saving to slit my wrist and went to work. I was not happy, but I did it anyway. I was so fortunate to have people around me that loved me. They kept giving me words of encouragement, but nothing was more motivating than the hard work I put in personally. It kept me busy producing and I couldn't be in my feelings. I worked like I never did before, long hours and lots of heads. I hired quickly to fill my chairs and held my breath. We got into the community and I worked my ass off. That is where the magic began to happen.

I started to research walkouts. As it turns out there is a silver lining with each walkout: fresh start or change for the better. You see, it is common for large salons to suffer this kind of loss and the rebound can be sweet. I had a glimpse of hope.

I began to envision how my new fresh Ringletts would operate. Little by little it became even better than it was before. I tweaked a few systems to ensure an exit plan for myself and someway, somehow, through the years I had planted enough seeds that it attracted the most amazing team members. I launched a hiring frenzy and I lucked up on some pretty dynamic hair stylists that were waiting to be Ringletts' girls. Ringletts' great reputation had preceded itself and it started to gain momentum once again. I got busy putting in the work. I had to trust and I did.

Today I have forgiven all the souls that walked out on me, because no weapon formed against me shall prosper. Just like a rose needs to be pruned to grow fuller blossoms, Ringletts needed pruning which was followed by amazing blossoms. Now I trust. I trust that God knew what He was doing. I trust that my work is good enough, I trust that my future is bright. I trust what I don't understand, and I trust what blessings are to come.

Success doesn't come easy, but I can honestly report that Ringletts makes well over ½ million dollars in sales per year and a second location has been launched in downtown New Orleans inside the Hilton Riverside hotel to fulfill the need of a different demographic. Clients are pouring in, phenomenal superstars, and team players fill up Ringletts today, and we are grooving once again! It is all because we are the home of respect, collaboration, education, happiness, and success.

What I Know For Sure:

-Visualization is powerful. Take time to just sit still, no TV, no computer, and no social media and visualize your dream.

Be specific; see yourself doing exactly what you want, down to the color of your shoes.

Right now, I am practicing the visualization of becoming a philanthropist because it makes me feel amazing to give and help those in need. The Lord knows I don't have the funds to be a heavy hitting money donator yet, but I go back to the drawing board to what I know to work, and I practice it. Stay tuned and let's see what happens...

-Fear will keep you from all your dreams. If you are aware that you are fearful of anything especially when it comes to your business, make a mental note to move through it. This will take a bit of bravery, but you can do it. It will give you a tremendous amount of elation and unspoken power to conquer it.

-**Business is about solving problems.** Business is about putting out fires as some may call it. Everyday I solve issues and I make a path out of a place where there is none. This is what a successful entrepreneur does.

- **Know how to execute.** Lots of people come up with good ideas. Hundreds of ideas per minute can be thought of, but to put something in motion and figure out how to make it go is of utmost importance. To witness it "go" is the sweet spot of business ownership. From conception to launching of any business- it takes focus and quiet research time to come to a conclusion of how to tackle each issue.

-**Listen to your gut**. I have never been the one to try to reinvent the wheel, but I have tweaked it a bit. Every single day I follow my gut. I get quiet and I listen to my deepest thoughts and feelings. I move on those feelings and if it doesn't feel right, I don't do it... period. I follow the beat of few people, but I listen to those who have carved their way before me and have something to show for it.

- **"There is more than one way to skin a cat"** is what I always tell my daughter. If we can just let ourselves get quiet. That means no TV, no computer, no phone, no noise and let God speak to us. He gives us simple solutions in our hearts, creativity to work around problems and a calm place to see our issues and solve them.

- **"If it doesn't make dollars, it doesn't make sense"**. It is very simple, but in the mumbo jumbo world of putting out fires in business, we can lose the "why" in the reason the business was launched. If you own a business that is for profit, there needs to be a profit. Otherwise your hard work is all for nothing.

-You don't have to spend a million dollars to look like a million dollars. With vision, style and a fashion sense, anyone can put together something great on a budget.

I have learned so many lessons on my journey as an entrepreneur. The biggest lesson I have learned and wish to share with all is to always let your thoughts come back to your deepest self, "your gut". Listen to what it tells you, this is where it all begins. In your journey you will experience high and lows, but your gut will always guide you.

ABOUT THE AUTHOR

Mindy, the fearless leader of Ringletts Salon, started her adventure in the hair industry thirty years ago. Today, she is the owner of one of the most vibrant businesses in New Orleans. Twelve years ago, "Ringletts Salon: was an idea in her head before she eventually went for her dreams. Mindy strives to make a difference in the life of both her clients and her stylists by teaching, mentoring and also learning from them at the same time. Ultimately, her goal is to make the entire experience all about the people that walk in the door. Mindy says, "Ringletts Salon has invested interest in the needs of each and every client, because each head of hair is unique."

Mindy is a Deva Curl Coach and she also believes that hair is a fabric, not a race and it should be understood by all her stylists. They should understand all from kinky to straight and from thin and fine to think and course. This is why she felt compelled to start Ringletts Salon.

Stay in touch with Mindy:
www.Ringletts.com
Instagram: @Ringletts
Facebook: @Ringletts

CHAPTER SEVEN

Nurse to Entrepreneur

Sonceria Roper

ENTREPRENEURSHIP: MY STORY, YOUR GUIDE

Entrepreneurship! I have always wanted to be an entrepreneur. Even at young age I knew that I wanted to call the shots; I just wasn't sure what path that I would take to get there. It has taken a long time to get where I am today, but I'm here!

For years I wasn't my best self; I was miserable working for other people and I couldn't figure out why. Part of my dismay was that as a nurse practitioner, I was tired of working under people that were less qualified than I was. One of my many breaking points was when I was working in a clinic seeing patients. The clinic manager, whom did not have medical knowledge nor experience, wanted to dictate how I should see my patients. I was completely out done by the audacity and his arrogance. To add insult to injury, the executive leadership (who also had no clinical experience) backed him. This was the beginning of the end for me. I decided that I was too smart for that type of situation.

In addition, I was unfulfilled and often wondered, "is this it?". I knew that my current situation was my life, but I was not living. I was overworked and too exhausted to actually enjoy the salary that I was making. It affected my time with family and my social life. On many occasions, I was forced to skip church to catch up with charting, I was snippy due to stress, and I was neglecting my health.

During this time, I also realized that no company would ever pay me what I was worth and that my salary would eventually cap. The thought of that frustrated me. As a single mother, I knew that I wanted to build generational wealth and leave my son with a legacy. I wanted my son to have opportunities that would set him up for success. I felt that the only way I could provide that was through entrepreneurship.

It had gotten so bad that I didn't care what type of business I owned, I just knew that I needed to be the captain of my own destiny. I knew this, but still for awhile I feared losing the security of my six- figure salary. However, after being laid off twice I was finally able to learn to no longer depend on anyone else to dictate how and when I ate.

Now, I am the administrator and owner of Clarke Home Care. It is a private duty, non-medical agency that is geared toward helping seniors and patients with disabilities remain living safely in their homes. We help them with daily living activities such as bathing, dressing, etc. Things that we can take for granted everyday are the things that my company helps seniors do with dignity.

The long-term care business is a billion-dollar industry. According to the CDC (Center of Disease Control), it is estimated that the amount spent annually on paid long-term care services are between $210.9 billion (O'Shaughnessy, 2014) and $317.1 billion a year (Colello, Mulvey, & Talaga, 2013). It will continue to grow because of all of the cutting-edge technology and advanced pharmacology that allows people to live longer lives. But quantity doesn't equal quality! Further, baby boomers are aging, but still want to maintain their dignity by staying in their own home. With a background in hospice and palliative care, I witnessed the needs that my senior patients had. It was upsetting to see that the quality of care that they were receiving from home care agencies, which was not personalized nor efficient. Out of that reason Clarke Home Care was birthed.

Clarke Home Care is not the first chapter of my entrepreneur story. I had tried the entrepreneur thing twice before and those ventures hadn't panned out. But this time I was determined to make the outcome different; it was do or die. I had a "50 cent" mentality: "Get rich or die trying."

This time I was doing something I knew and loved-healthcare. Everything that I had done in my career, learned in school, and experienced through my other ventures had prepared me for this venture. Clarke Home Care is not my side hustle, it is my main hustle. It has been the most freeing experience in my life. No one else's business comes before my business. It is my second baby and I'm a proud mama!

My Story:

A little about me: I was born in Houston, Texas, which is also where I currently reside. I am my parents' youngest child and grew up being encouraged to do well in school. For the most part I managed to stay on the straight and narrow and graduated college with my Bachelors in Nursing. After a few years of working as an RN, I started to have that itch that there had to be more to my career than being on my feet for twelve hours non-stop. In 2006, I entered graduate school to see if that would offer career advancement and job satisfaction. I graduated in 2009 with my Masters of Nursing and started my career as a Nurse Practitioner. I enjoyed that role for a few years and still currently practice on an as needed basis providing hospice and palliative care services to patients. However, I couldn't shake my longing to be an entrepreneur. Little by little, before and after work, I would do something daily to get closer to my goal of being an entrepreneur.

The biggest concerns for me, as it is for many entrepreneurs, was not my ability and my expertise, but funding and effective marketing.

Funding:

I personally funded my start-up business cost. I used my personal savings (which might not have been the smartest move looking back). I wouldn't recommend it because it's too risky and can leave you in a financial bind especially if it takes your business a while to become profitable There are going to be so many frustrating moments when you begin, save yourself some heartache by not adding your personal finances to it. Every time I got paid, I would buy something for my business. Little by little I built my business off of credit cards and my personal earnings. I also started re-evaluating what was essential and what was not. Little non-essentials, such as Netflix and Starbucks, had to go. Every little bit adds up and counts toward my goal. I have sold personal items and used tax return funds to invest in my business.

When you really want something, you are willing to make the sacrifices. When I was eliminating some of the non- essentials and selling personal items, I was thinking about the bigger picture. I was thinking about the huge gain that I would have after the short- term sacrifice. I bet on myself and it paid off!

Not everyone can or wants to take this route. There are other options to funding your entrepreneur dreams. Small business loans are one option. However, most require that you are already generating revenue with your business. To avoid this, you can apply for a personal loan. Depending on the type of business that you would like to start, there may be grants available to cover startup cost. Some business owners borrow against their 401k or take a line of credit from their homes. Everyone's situation is different. Each entrepreneur must determine what will work best in their situation. The most important thing to remember is that if one way does not work, it does not mean that you should quit. It just means that you have to find a different way. Once you determine how to "fund it out", you have to then get the word out.

Marketing:

When it came to getting the word out and marketing my business, I knew I had to determine my niche. I also had to determine what would separate me from the next business owner in my field. I needed people to see why they should do business with me instead of an industry giant that had already gained trust and familiarity. One of my favorite movies is "Coming to America". In the movie Mr. McDowell owned a fast food restaurant that sold hamburgers that was eerily similar to McDonalds. There's one scene in the movie that he stated that what made him different was that they (McDonalds) had the "Golden Arches" while he had the "Golden Arc". For myself, I promote my education as a nurse practitioner when I'm pitching to potential clients in order to differentiate myself from competitors. A lot of home care agencies aren't owned by health care workers so I leverage that to my advantage. Clients tend to feel more comfortable with someone who has experience. I also promote free fall risk assessments instead of a free in-home assessment like my competitors. Falls can be detrimental to the health of seniors, so this definitely catches the attention of clients. You must ask yourself, what need will your business fill in order to find your niche.

In order to be successful, you must get your business in front of people that you don't know you. Friends and family are only going to purchase so many goods and services. This won't sustain your business. Someone new needs to learn about your business every day in order to grow. In order to reach these people, my advice is to have a separate budget specifically for marketing. One thing that I did not factor in when starting my business was the cost of marketing. I totally underestimated that part. Being that my budget was small, I did lots of budget shopping and comparing of marketing companies. I encourage you to do the same and make sure you're getting a good ROI (Return on Investment) for your marketing dollars.

In addition to obtaining marketing services, you can also be your own billboard! Wearing a shirt with your logo is a great conversation piece and a way to spark up a conversation about your business. OPEN YOUR MOUTH. Don't be afraid to talk about your business anywhere and to everyone that will listen. You never know what door that will open. Play yourself up! This once was a struggle for me. Most people don't know that I'm naturally shy. I'm pretty reserved and I have never been a social butterfly. This takes practice and prayer; I literally prayed for confidence. I would have my pitch written and would study it so that I could articulate myself well and would not sound foolish in front of potential clients and referral sources.

As a home care agency owner, you have to build a strong referral source in order to continue to have new clients. Patients move, pass away, or just no longer need services. Therefore, you must always have potential clients ready to replace them. Great referral sources are physician offices, hospitals, nursing rehab facilities, assisted living facilities, and hospice companies. You have to become best friends with case managers in order to get those referrals going. Consistent communication with these referral sources is essential because when they have patients that need in home care, you want your company to be the first agency that comes to mind.

I would also encourage business owners to get out in the community and possibly even be a vendor at an event. I do not encourage jumping at every opportunity. It is equally as important to be strategic. In remaining strategic, I only market at events that tie into what my business is about. For example, I was a vendor at a race event to prevent colon cancer. It was a perfect place to market in front of clinicians, families, and patients needing care. Think about the opportunity and if you would connect with either great referral sources or with potential clients. If you can't make the connections then it likely would not be worth your time. Time is money! Only give your time to things that will benefit your business; you cannot be everywhere.

Most importantly as an entrepreneur it is important to remain consistent. Keep showing up at the right events, keep wearing your shirts with your logo, keep giving out marketing material. It is also key to keep reaching out to new clients. Don't worry about being a pest. I went to a hospice facility three times before I started receiving any patient referrals. People need to know that you're serious. Also, it builds relationships and trust and makes people want to refer you. Also, don't underestimate the power of networking. I promise that you will meet someone that needs your services. You can be of service to other business owners by referring business to them- they will appreciate it and return the favor.

Multiple Streams of Income:

As an entrepreneur, I am constantly trying to monetize my talents. I intentionally follow millionaires on social media and read books written by them. I do this because that's my goal; I want to be a millionaire. One thing that I learned that all have in common is that they all have several sources of incomes. So, when one business may not be meeting its quarterly goals, they have other revenue that is being generated in order to make up for the deficit.

In order to generate multiple streams, I not only market to individuals but I have also bid on state and government contracts. Additionally, I'm always looking for additional services that I can offer my clients in order to bring in more income.

My Mistakes:

After about almost a year in business things started to pick up for me. I started receiving more leads for clients and I had the most clients that I ever had on my roster; things were great. Suddenly, Hurricane Harvey hit in Houston, Texas where I reside. Fortunately, I did not lose my home like my Houstonians had; however, my business was impacted heavily. Many of my clients had been displaced and I was unable to service them. It became emotionally and financially devastating.

It may sound strange, but that situation turned into a blessing. The down time in my business let me take a step back and re-evaluate processes and practices that needed to change. The changes that I implemented has helped my business immensely. For one, I realized that I was letting my clients run too much of my business. I had been allowing my clients to pay late, negotiate prices, change my employees' schedule every week- all which would cause me to come out of my own pocket to keep my business afloat. I no longer permit that and the changes have made my life much easier and more convenient as a business owner.

An additional change which has been beneficial is that I now set a minimum of twenty hours a week for clients that we service. Previously I was forced to give my staff only two or four hours per week here or there. It had become frustrating trying to find quality team members that would work those hours. Further, the amount of work that it required to keep a patient serviced just did not make it worthwhile.

I also changed the manner in which I was accepting payments. I work with a lot of elderly patients who aren't computer savvy; it was hard for them to pay online. Instead I would allow them to mail in a check for their payments. I learned the hard way that this method was ineffective! They rarely paid on time and it was a headache. I started direct billing with a credit card on file once the payments became due. I no longer have issues with receiving timely payments.

This last business practice that I implemented was hard for me, but it was necessary. The lesson learned: NEVER NEGOTIATE YOUR PRICES. Your price is your price, period. If they can't afford your prices, they need to go somewhere else. This was hard for me because I'm a nurturer and I want to genuinely help people. But I had to realize that I was only cheating myself when I gave people a discount. To add more insult to injury, those that received discounts were typically the worse clients to deal with. The biggest lesson that I learned is that you don't need fifty clients. You need five -ten consistent clients that want your services and can afford you. I promise you, their money will make-up for the fifty that want to nickle and dime you.

Lastly, you need a mentor and a power partner in your field. This will save you time, money, and frustration. The knowledge that a mentor can share is invaluable. They have already made the mistakes that you can avoid. A power partner is someone who owns the same exact business that you do. Don't look at them as competitors. Trust me, they have information that you need. This has been effective for me because it has not only helped me make vital changes to my business practices, but also has led to referrals.

In conclusion, some of the best advice that I can give is to just start. Do one thing everyday toward your business and you'll be surprised how much you'll accomplish in six months just by starting today. Things aren't going to be perfect, but the beauty is that it doesn't have to be. It's your business so you set the rules. Don't allow employees and/ or customers dictate how you run your business. You took the leap to be an entrepreneur. That means that you're the boss and you make the rules. Don't waiver from that! Remember that entrepreneurship is a marathon not a sprint.

ABOUT THE AUTHOR

Sonceria Roper is a board- certified Nurse Practitioner and owner of Clarke Home Care in Houston, Texas. She has over thirteen years of nursing experience and is currently working on her doctorate degree in nursing at Prairie View A&M University. Her vast nursing experience includes surgery, retail, home health, teaching, and hospice. She currently resides in Houston, Texas with her son.

Stay in touch with Sonceria:

www.clarkehomecare.com

info@clarkehomecare.

CHAPTER EIGHT
Phenomenally Me

Patrina Dixon

ENTREPRENEURSHIP: MY STORY, YOUR GUIDE

My Story:

We all have stories about how we became who we are. When you hear stories of others you can learn new ways of creating a business and shaping your own narrative so that you too may one day tell a story of your own. For entrepreneurs, these stories often are success stories, and mine is no different.

Some people are born to do business, but do not realize it until they are presented with an opportunity. I think it's much the same way with anyone who suddenly encounters their calling, whether they are an entrepreneur, an artist, or an athlete. Something sparks the notion that this right for them; that this is what they should do. For me that moment came when I was a sophomore in high school and it was associated mostly with lollipops.

When I was a sophomore in high school my mom would bring home these big and colorful lollipops and other types of cool candy. She would bring home more candy than I could not possibly eat! I decided to bring some of the candy to school with me one day.

That day, while I was sitting in the lunchroom, another student approached me and asked me about my eye-catching candy. She offered me fifty cents for one of my big lollipops. It made me think: even though it was only fifty cents, I didn't pay anything to get the lollipop in the first place. It seemed like a good deal and I definitely liked the idea. I hesitated for a couple of seconds and then agreed to my first business transaction. It was the start of my journey in business, and it all started thanks to a colorful lollipop!

It could have stopped there, but it didn't. Later, a friend of that same student also asked me for a lollipop in exchange for fifty cents. Then another person and another. If you are not a true entrepreneur you're probably thinking I could have easily just given those lollipops away. But at that moment the entrepreneur spirit inside of me had awakened, saw an opportunity, and seized.

The candy sales were my first hustle or, should I say, my first business! When I got home I started to put this sweet enterprise together. I gathered all the lollipops and candy we had in the house. I also asked my mom and other relatives for more candy. I made a lot of money as a high school student as I became known as the "Candy Girl" in my school. It was a success path that started with lollipops. I sold lollipops for the rest of my time as a student. I would cycle my profits back into my supply and then treat myself to something small every week.

ENTREPRENEURSHIP: MY STORY, YOUR GUIDE

This was the start of my journey, but it was far from the end. The candy business was the foundation for my current business. It taught me many things which I still apply in my professional life. First, I learned that I could make money by providing a solution and responding to what others needed. The kids in my school wanted candy, which they couldn't buy in the cafeteria and which many of their parents did not provide. My peers wanted more of what I had to offer; my products were in demand. It also taught me some basic ideas of business, like what making a profit meant. It also showed me how within a business you need strong allies to support you. My allies were my family as they helped by initially providing the candy.

Soon after high school, however, I had to focus on something else. I became pregnant with my beautiful daughter and later became a single mom. This was a hard job for me; one I often refer to as my own "School of Hard Knocks"! I worked hard to raise my daughter. It was important for me to ensure she had not just her basic needs, but a decent standard of life. Although it was an enormous amount of responsibility, I learned the meaning of sacrifice. Becoming a parent showed me how to put someone's needs before mine, but still prioritize my own.

While I still wanted to be an entrepreneur, I put that dream on hold because I needed a steady paycheck and medical insurance for the two of us. I never lost that dream, but I did put it off because it was best for my daughter at the time.

For the next few years I worked different jobs until I finally landed a job at a large insurance company. Twenty-three years later I am the Senior National Accounts Manager for that same company. Despite having this amazing and stable position, I still did not give up on my dream. Even though stability was essential component in my life, I still believed I needed to have my own business and help others in the process. I wanted more. Because of these feelings I decided to have both: a career and my own business.

This was the start of a business project that I am proud to say today is a reality. As the Owner and CEO and founder of P. Dixon Consulting, we focus on providing personal financial services. My service to the community is showcased in my speaking engagements, volunteer events, and the release of my journal series, "It'$ My Money". The series provides financial education to people of all ages on their road to financial independence and success. Each volume addresses a specific age group and the common financial issues pertaining to that segment of life.

Financial literacy is important to me. The entrepreneurial spirit within allowed me to start the candy business, but it also wanted to help others discover their own inner entrepreneur spirit. So, it became vital for me to assist with spreading knowledge of financial management and giving others the tools to continually grow and enter entrepreneurship.

I chose to be an entrepreneur because I wanted to be my own boss. The allure of such freedom, responsibility, and creation was enough for me. I knew that mostly all major decisions would be up to me as it pertained to projects, partnerships, and direction. It is important to me to offer opportunities to those who are having difficulty finding employment. This is something I want embedded into my business practices. I envisioned, with such vision and drive that my network would increase, my expertise would be showcased, and my passion could now become a profit.

In a lot of ways, my decision to become an entrepreneur was driven by who I am and how I conduct myself. I am naturally inquisitive and I love to explore different topics. There's always been a deep love for creativity, innovation and culture. Manifesting tools that are useful for others is practical and personal. No one wants something in which they cannot find purpose. As an entrepreneur, I can blend all of these concepts. Most importantly I now understand how my childhood experiences, journey to motherhood, stable career, and family has prepared me for entrepreneurship. All along I've had to manage finances and have provided support for others. I actually enjoyed doing it all. In my business, I am simply sharing my experiences and practical tools and techniques with others. My business, has offered a chance for me to capitalize from skills and practices that I love.

There were several things I implemented which were vital to my business dreams becoming a reality. I will share them with you in the hopes that it will help you grow:

6. Consulting and Feedback:

As I continued to develop my business plans, before I could truly make the leap of faith, I needed to consult my family. In addition to becoming a mother, I had also become a wife. The vital roles of motherhood and family were foundations of my success. It was only right for me to seek their approval and support. As I sat down with my husband it was reassuring to hear him express his unconditional support. More than anything, it was important for him to witness me pursue my dreams without compromising. Next, I consulted with my mother and daughter. We talked about my goals and vision collectively as a family. They too, were enthusiastic about the journey ahead. Looking back, I am still grateful for how positive, encouraging, and uplifting they were.

After sharing my plans with my family, I sought out a few individuals for their feedback, mentorship, and outside support. I wanted to explore my business plan with others, to hear commentary on whether they thought it would work. Luckily, I received an array of feedback. Some trustworthy individuals told me it was a solid plan because many people needed help with their finances. I also presented the idea for the book and received plenty of feedback stating that many kids needed that type of guidance. The best advice given was to follow my dreams, have a plan, and always know your field. However, not all of the feedback that I received was stellar; nonetheless it was helpful. While the positive advice and responses fueled my confidence, the constructive commentary sparked small changes and tweaks to my business plan.

I was amazed to find so many people willing to support and help me. People would offer their thoughts, views, and opinions on how to proceed with projects. I've maintained tremendous appreciation towards everyone. In the end, however, all the decisions were up to me. I had to make the choices that made sense and that fit my vision.

2. Speaking and Writing:

I immediately began moving forward with my plan. I started small by volunteering for speaking engagements. I started this way because I understood that I would need to cultivate a brand and name for myself within the financial literacy industry to be a success. Volunteering to share my knowledge helped me to do just that. Simultaneously I began the process of logo creation, creating business cards and working with a web designer to create a website that reflected my vision and the mission of the business.

I officially launched my business in March of 2016. In September of the same year, I also published the first of three in the *It'$ My Money* journal series. With the release of the financial literacy journal series underway, I could now place author on my list of accomplishments. By January of 2017 Volume 1 was translated into Spanish, thereby expanding my reach to another audience. I also further expanded my reach by making the book available as a digital resource with a modified e-book version.

Becoming a published author was yet another step on my journey as an entrepreneur. It was challenging, but it was also incredibly rewarding. The book is a collection of my desires and knowledge. It has been a platform for me to share material that inspires me in ways that can also inspire others. The process was something I could have completed by myself; but instead chose to employ a team. I had an editor to review my writing, a designer for the book cover, an attorney for legal documents, and of course the support from my family all played a role on its completion. The evolution of my support system and professional network cultivated some of my greatest ideas.

3. Funding and Finances:

Before launching I had to save money and did so by having a fixed amount go into a savings account automatically. This was important because I used some of my savings to fund my business. When profits were generated in the business I funneled them back into the business. I also used different strategies for the funding, many of which I like to share with others. Using several banking accounts for the business is a practice I adopted after reading *Profit First* by Mike Michalowicz. Most importantly I take it one day at a time – having a business isn't a sprint, it is a journey. Starting out it was vital for longevity and my own financial management to work within my budget. Taking on projects that are within my professional means and seeking services that were within my personal budget was necessary. Over time, these decisions were proven to be smart as I saw my profits increase. I can finally testify that my company is self-sustaining and producing a profit. It took me about a year to save to start my own business and a little over a year to start to see some profit. There were many times I felt discouraged but remember why I got started and my great supports were always there cheering me one.

4. Marketing:

Through trial and error, I soon found one of the most important aspects of entrepreneurship is marketing. Initially, I did not budget enough funds for advertisements and marketing. As you've likely heard: it takes money to make money. However, in the process I did learn that promoting to your target audience and new individuals is the key to longevity and sustainability within a business. Because of my mistake, I started my company with a lot of self-promotion. Serving as my own cheerleader and handling the day to day was difficult, but it was a pinnacle lesson of sacrifice.

I knew that I wanted to engage my audience and provide information at the same time. I felt as though my company website was key. With the website, I could communicate with followers on the blog, showcase the book, and offer my professional services. It provides potential clients all the information they need about my services. The content is regularly updated and it gets people interested in my book and eventually draws in new clients. Given the fact that I didn't have a marketing budget, I depended on my network through text and email to offer feedback and to promote the content on my website.

I depended on my network to do the same thing upon the release of my book. In addition to the support of my network I also visited several local bookstores, asking the owner for an opportunity to showcase the journal series. The responses have been a part of the journey. Every "yes" or "no" is still a lesson of learning as I walk this path of entrepreneurship. In addition to acquiring locations for sales,

I worked tirelessly to secure a variety of book signing events. No matter the size, I needed the practice. Because of such humility, I've had the pleasure of participating in several events at local bookstores, libraries, and professional conferences.

Marketing the book became a priority as the book was also a means to market my services through the text of the book. Additionally, The sales of the book and journals are a source of income in addition to my professional services. The books and journals have served as a fuel for my spark and it continues to motivate me on my journey.

5. Relationship Building:

Cultivating experiences and building relationships has become an essential component of my success. Having the courage to not only promote myself, but to also make new connections in the process continually expands my personal reach and professional audience. All the steps I've taken thus far have led to my entrepreneurial success. I've traveled to other cities and states as a result of such labor. I attended tons of local networking events, big and small, and traveled for a few that I believed would be beneficial to my journey. I have met a ton of people at these events and some have translated into paid clients and some have been possible collaborations. I have also learned from some of the people I meet. I always carry and share, strategically, my business card and the cards I collect, I make it a point to reach out. The next steps depend on the contact, their business, and how I see us working together or learning from each other.

6. Branding:

As an entrepreneur, you are your brand. No matter where I go, I represent P. Dixon Consulting. Furthermore, the journal series, *It'$ My Money*, has also become its own brand. I have websites and social media platforms that allow me to reach my target audience daily for both projects. I utilize the blog to share resourceful information pertaining to financial tips, money management, opportunities, and more. Cross branding my products and professional services expands my reach domestically and internationally.

6. Other Tips:

Overall, I know my first year of entrepreneurship has been one full of ambition, growth, and promise. My journey's taken me farther than I could have imagined, but I still have a way to go. I am a mother, wife, and businesswoman all while maintaining a career. I've turned my passions into profits. I've found a way to give back to my community while still educating, offering, and increasing financial literacy programs. We aid small businesses, provide financial coaching, credit restoration services, book clubs and financial literacy workshops. P. Dixon Consulting aims to be a pillar within the money management industry. The stability of my professional career provides financial flexibility so I can run my personal business. Blending the two together is what makes my road to entrepreneurship so unique. Most people believe you must drop all your priorities, quit your day job, and dedicate yourself 100% to your company to truly be an entrepreneur. This is not true. If anything, it is more challenging finding discipline and maintaining the passion behind all your decisions when coupled with a busy career.

If you are currently contemplating or are maintaining entrepreneurship while still employed full time, just know that there will be moments when you'd rather focus on your entrepreneur endeavors. There will be times when you see the fruit of your labor and contemplate walking away from your career. There will also be moments when you're wondering when things will fall into place and you may feel discouraged. But know, chasing your dreams and accomplishing your goals is never an easy task. I am here to tell you that the journey is worth the reward.

Never sell yourself short. Define success for yourself and reach for it. Anything imaginable can be created. Do the work. Reflect on what you're passionate about and create a plan to manifest that greatness throughout your life. The key is developing a plan but remaining flexible throughout the journey. Understand that with freedom comes responsibility, and for your company to thrive you must maintain discipline. Do your research and know your target market. Create a business plan. Review it. Revise it. Write it again. Take feedback. Rage at the feedback. Fix it again until you have a working project. Take notes, write down your goals, and review them everyday. If you believe in yourself, others will too. Build up your confidence and strengthen your resources. Become the professional others can trust. Stay up to date on things in your field and your market. Train. Learn. Grow. Be sure to have money for marketing! Be willing to push through adversity along the journey.

My mission is to help young people and their families all over the world to be more financially astute. What is your mission? What will be your journey? What story do you want to tell

ABOUT THE AUTHOR

Patrina Dixon, Certified Financial Education Instructor and award- winning author of top-selling financial guided series, "It'$ My Money™" is an advocate for financial literacy. Patrina has a passion for serving her community and uses her company, P. Dixon Consulting, LLC to offer money management strategies to people of all ages. She led Hartford's Financially Fit community event and enjoyed her role as a Personal Finance volunteer for Junior Achievement. Patrina is shaping the spending and saving behaviors of her clients with a goal of guiding them toward financial independence.

Through her education received at the University of Hartford's Barney School of Business, as a proud mom and a life-long financial advisor – she understands and thrives at teaching the importance of financial literacy. Patrina also holds a Financial Management Certificate from Cornell University. The It'$ My Money™ journal series, workshops and book clubs allows Patrina to educate and enlighten families on their finances. She is dedicated to molding the next set of financial leaders. Patrina is a devoted wife and mother who resides in Connecticut.

Stay in touch with Patrina:
www.Itsmymoneyjournal.info
Instagram: @Itsmymoney_
Facebook: @Itsmymoneyjournal

www.ingramcontent.com/pod-product-compliance
Lightning Source LLC
Chambersburg PA
CBHW050217230526
45470CB00001B/434